"Then **Steve** Said to **Jerry**…"

The Best San Francisco 49ers Stories Ever Told

Steve Silverman

TRIUMPH
BOOKS

Library of Congress Cataloging-in-Publication Data

Silverman, Steve, 1956–
 "Then Steve said to Jerry": the best San Francisco 49ers stories ever told / Steve Silverman.
    p. cm.
 ISBN-13: 978-1-60078-094-3
 ISBN-10: 1-60078-094-6
 1. San Francisco 49ers (Football team)—History. I. Title.
 GV956.S3S55 2008
 796.332'640979461—dc22
                                          2008021091

This book is available in quantity at special discounts for your group or organization. For further information, contact:

Triumph Books
542 South Dearborn Street
Suite 750
Chicago, Illinois 60605
(312) 939-3330
Fax (312) 663-3557

Printed in U.S.A.
ISBN: 978-1-60078-094-3
Design by Patricia Frey
All photos courtesy of AP Images unless unless otherwise indicated.

Content packaged by Mojo Media, Inc.
Joe Funk: Editor
Jason Hinman: Creative Director

To Samantha and Gregory.
You are always in my heart and soul.

table of
CONTENTS

Foreword

Being a professional football player was anything but easy. While today I may be in the Hall of Fame, and I threw six touchdown passes in the Super Bowl, every day was a struggle. Why? When you are a quarterback and you want to play in the NFL and you are backing up Joe Montana, the chances of getting into the lineup are not good.

When that chance finally comes, everything is going to be measured by how Joe did it. If that's not bad enough, try playing quarterback in the NFL when you are just six feet tall and you have to throw the ball over the outstretched arms of men who are four, five, and six inches taller than you.

But once that opportunity comes, you can't think about all the things working against you. It's more about taking advantage of that opportunity, even if circumstances seem to be against you. After coming to the 49ers from the Tampa Bay Bucs, there were a lot of trials and tough moments, but ultimately I couldn't have asked for a better place to be. I got to work with Bill Walsh, one of the brightest minds the game has ever known. My teammates included Joe Montana and Ronnie Lott. I got to throw the ball to Jerry Rice, the greatest receiver to play the game.

There were moments of struggle, but when we won the Super Bowl following the 1994 season against the Chargers and I got to throw that monkey off my back, it was an unreal feeling. At the same time that huge burden was finally being lifted, I was also celebrating the greatest accomplishment a football player could hope to have. I'm not talking about being named MVP—I'm talking about winning the Super Bowl. Words still don't do it justice.

But in addition to film and videotape, words are what we have left to describe what we went through in our careers. In this book, veteran NFL writer Steve Silverman takes a long look at the 49ers and what they mean to the NFL, their fans, and the American sporting public. He takes us on a journey from the early days of the organization and through the magical era orchestrated by Bill Walsh that lasted the better part of two decades. It is a story he tells with passion and skill. It is the story of a great team—and era—told in a way that brings it back to life.

—Steve Young

Acknowledgments

Playing pro sports for a living may be about the best way to make a living, but writing about sports is not a bad way to go either.

The switch was flipped for me at the age of eight, when I became aware of the thrill of competition and the wonders of pro sports. It started during the 1964 World Series, when I saw Mickey Mantle hit a game-winning home run in the bottom of the ninth inning. My interests soon included football as well.

Jim Brown, Bart Starr, and Dick Butkus were my heroes and the complexity and color of the sport were amazing. The charisma of a head coach like Vince Lombardi and a quarterback like Joe Namath only intensified my interest.

Throughout my high school and college years I could never conceive of doing anything other than writing about sports for a living. My first experience at covering the game was for a medium-sized paper in New Brunswick, New Jersey, called the *Home News*. I was a young sportswriter, and the sports editor called a meeting in the fall of 1981. He laid out the expectations of the sports department and the newspaper's rules and regulations. As the meeting was about to end, he said he had one other piece of business. "We are covering the Giants," he lamented. "Does anyone want to cover the game this week?"

My hand couldn't go up fast enough. To think that such an opportunity was presented as if it were a burden was amazing.

Nobody else wanted the gig. I covered the Giants against the St. Louis Cardinals that fall Sunday in 1981 and many of the other Giants games as well. Lawrence Taylor was a rookie, Bill Parcells was an assistant coach, and Phil Simms was struggling with inconsistency. The Giants made the playoffs that season for the first time in 18 years, and it was sheer excitement when they beat the Cowboys in the season finale on a field goal by Joe Danelo in overtime. The franchise was on its way to a return to glory.

A few years later I became immersed in my career while working for Hub Arkush at *Pro Football Weekly*. Along with writers and editors like Rick Korch, Bob LeGere, Michael Lev, Ron Pollack, Neil Warner, Keith Schleiden, Dan Arkush, and the late Joel Buchsbaum, I worked on a great paper that remains so to this day.

The Sporting News editor Scott Smith has allowed me to be a part of his fine magazines including NFL, college football, and fantasy football previews. MSNBC.com's George Malone and Mike Miller have also given me a forum that I truly appreciate.

Colleagues like Allen Barra and Allen St. John have given me an opportunity to expand my horizons and improve my craft. Both are outstanding writers and good friends.

Triumph Books editor Tom Bast has given me a chance to write this book on a tremendous subject like the 49ers. Doing the research on this legendary team led me to reconnect with Joe Horrigan of the NFL Hall of Fame along with that institution's Pete Fierle and Saleem Choudhry.

Finally, a big squeeze to my daughter Samantha and my son Gregory. You are both my bright lights and my pride and joy. You are both the best things ever to happen to me.

Introduction

What an opportunity.

Not just for the 49ers, who had the opportunity to dominate the NFL for the better part of two decades, but for any writer associated with this team.

During my 10-year stint at *Pro Football Weekly*, I had the chance to write about the 49ers nearly every week and talk with those who were with the team and cover it on a regular basis.

In addition to building a winning organization, the Niners had one of the most cerebral teams in sports history. Former head coach and leader Bill Walsh wanted his team to win, but it wasn't just a matter of taking their opponents out in the back alley and beating them up. Walsh wanted to outsmart them and outtechnique them as well.

Not instead of, but in addition to.

The image of Walsh is that he wanted to outfinesse his opponent and sip wine while he was doing it. At least that's the image that some of his critics want to believe. That image—the sweatered Walsh with his hand resting on his chin like some modern version of Rodin's *Thinker*—is nothing but a cliché, and a false one at that.

He had a brilliant offense with leaders like Joe Montana and Steve Young, and he used their talents to confound opponents. But he also had a defense that featured Ronnie Lott and Fred Dean, and neither one of those Hall of Famers were known for their subtlety. They both hit like rushing freight trains, and they dominated with physical play.

This is the story of a Niners team that was so good during the

1980s that the 1984 and 1989 teams are often mentioned with the '70's Steelers, 1972 Dolphins, and 1985 Chicago Bears as the best the game has ever seen.

"Then Steve Said to Jerry..." is the story of the franchise's many ups and few downs during those years, with the prior and future years used as depth. The 49ers wrote the book on consistency and domination, always playing with an intellectual edge that was punctuated by physical domination.

Steve Young probably represents what this franchise is about as well as anybody. A dominant athlete—who could have been a fine running back if he didn't throw the football as well as anybody who ever played the game—Young had the heavy responsibility of following Joe Montana in the Niners scheme. While he had all the talent in the world and was considered open, fair-minded, and communicative with the fans and media, he was welcomed with all the warmth of a second-story burglar who comes in through the transom.

He didn't do anything wrong, he just wasn't Montana.

All Young ever did for the Niners was win, and he was finally welcomed as a conquering hero when he brought home the franchise's fifth Super Bowl title following the 1994 season. He did it with the help of Brent Jones, Ricky Watters, John Taylor, a great group of blockers, and an underrated defense. However, his most important partner in that endeavor was Jerry Rice, and this is their story.

The Niners were a team that had it all: an offense for the ages; a great but little-appreciated defensive unit; brilliant coaching and tons of memorable moments.

Some of those moments were in the Super Bowl, where the Niners won all five of the opportunities they had. They handled the pressure as big favorites over the Broncos and as underdogs in their first against the Bengals.

They came of age against the Cowboys, a team that had tortured them in a previous generation. The Niners also finished their run with another NFC title game win over the Cowboys.

The never-ending argument that all football fans have is which was the best football team of all time. The four teams who are in the discussion are the 1972–73 Dolphins, the 1970s Steelers, the

1985 Bears, and the great Niners teams. Most experts eliminate the Dolphins and the Bears in the first round of cuts, leaving the Steelers and Niners to fight for the overall title.

No argument there, because that's just how we see it. The Steelers have the defensive edge, the Niners have the offensive advantage. In the final analysis it may be the coaching. Chuck Noll was an awesome leader for the Steelers, but he lacked the creativity and imagination of Walsh—and that could well be the deciding factor.

Chapter 1
The Years Before Walsh

The 49ers always belonged to San Francisco. They weren't somebody else's rejects who happened to move to the beautiful city by the bay.

The Good, Old Days

They have been the most beloved sports team ever in the city of San Francisco.

That's because the 49ers always belonged to the city. They weren't somebody else's rejects who happened to move to the beautiful city by the bay. The Giants belonged to New York City until Horace Stoneham decided he was tired of playing third fiddle in a city with three baseball teams. The Warriors were Philadelphia's beloved team for many years before making their way west. The San Jose Sharks? They're in San Jose—for the love of Mike! They also started playing, oh, about the day before yesterday.

The Niners played in the All-America Football Conference from 1946 through 1949 and were one of three teams that merged into the NFL following the 1949 season, joined by the Cleveland Browns and Baltimore Colts. The Niners quickly became contenders in the NFL, finishing with a winning record from 1951 through 1954.

Over the years, the team developed many star players who became fan favorites. In the early years, it started with quarterback Frankie Albert. The records show Albert was 5'10" and 166 pounds, but he was more like 5'8" and 155. He looked more like a water boy than a quarterback, but he was an excellent signal caller with a penchant for making big plays.

Albert made the 1951 Pro Bowl team and in subsequent years the Niners would send defensive tackle Leo Nomellini, fullback Joe "the Jet" Perry, halfback Hugh McElhenny, quarterback Y.A. Tittle, and a ferocious offensive tackle in Bob St. Clair.

The Niners also had another player in flankerback R.C. Owens, who was among the most exciting in football. Owens was a 6'3" leaping machine who could easily propel himself over the top of opposing defensive backs. Tittle took advantage of his extraordinary leaping ability by throwing him high passes that only Owens could come down with. The "Alley-Oop" plays became Owens's signature and nickname.

R.C. Owens demonstrates his Alley-Oop catch for the camera during workout at Redwood City, California, in November 1957. Play-acting defense against the pass are Paul Carr, left, and Dicky Moegle. Three times in 1957 Owens came up with the catch to win games—the last time against Detroit in the final 11 seconds of play.

In addition to being wildly entertaining, the Alley-Oop plays became the foundation for using bigger wide receivers who could leap over smaller defensive backs. Those plays are in nearly every NFL offense more than 50 years later.

Throughout the 1960s the Niners were usually a very respectable team, with six out of 10 seasons at .500 or better, but they never came close to winning an NFL Western Conference title.

But the parade of top-level players—particularly on the offensive side—continued. Start with quarterback John Brodie, who had one of the smoothest releases and most accurate deliveries of any quarterback of that generation. While Johnny Unitas of the Colts and Bart Starr of the Packers were the greatest quarterbacks of that decade, both men often talked about Brodie when the subject was quarterbacks they admire.

Brodie had two fine running backs in halfback John David Crow and fullback Ken Willard, and receivers Dave Parks and Gene Washington baffled defensive backs. The name Howard Mudd is familiar to NFL fans as the offensive line coach of the Indianapolis Colts, but he was a Pro Bowl blocker in San Francisco as was center Bruce Bosley.

The Niners were not bereft of defensive talent either. Cornerbacks Jimmy Johnson and Kermit Alexander were both sensational cover men who were also big-time hitters. They also had a linebacker in Dave "the Intimidator" Wilcox, who may have been as violent and nasty as Ray Nitschke or Dick Butkus.

The Niners upped their status in the early 1970s when they won the NFC West title in the first year of the decade to earn their first postseason victory since joining the NFL. They couldn't have drawn a tougher opponent than the Minnesota Vikings, who at that time were the dreaded Purple People Eaters and played in frozen Metropolitan Stadium.

Pass rushers Jim Marshall, Carl Eller, and Alan Page were supposed to eat Brodie for lunch, but the Niners came away with a 17–14 upset. A 17–10 loss to the Cowboys in the NFC Championship Game hurt badly, but the season was clearly a positive one.

Despite a respectable 17-year career at quarterback, John Brodie and the 49ers were mostly unsuccessful in the1960s and 1970s. This picture shows Brodie leaving the game against the Pittsburgh Steelers in San Francisco on December 17, 1973. It was Brodie's final game, as he had announced his retirement earlier in the season.

The Niners defended their division title each of the next two seasons but lost to the Cowboys in the postseason. That was it for the glory years until new owner Eddie DeBartolo Jr. hired a coach named Bill Walsh in 1979.

That move would key the Niners' rise from a football afterthought to one of the great franchises in sports history.

Hitting Rock Bottom

The 49ers have a great legacy in the NFL and they may be the best team that ever played the game. Five Super Bowl championships in the 1980s and 1990s put San Francisco at the top of the heap with the Pittsburgh Steelers, and both the 1984 and 1994 teams get regular consideration for being the best individual teams to ever play football.

But make no mistake about it, life was not always grand for the 49ers. They were weak stepsisters in the NFL for decades, getting bludgeoned regularly by their archrival Los Angeles Rams and losing the battle for popularity with the Oakland Raiders across the bay.

When Bill Walsh was hired in 1979, the 49ers had finally made the move that got the franchise on the right track, but the mood of the team and the outlook for the future was never worse than just before he was hired.

Monte Clark became head coach after the Niners fired Dick Nolan at the end of the 1975 season. Clark had earned the position as an assistant coach under Don Shula in Miami. Shula had been Clark's boss and mentor, telling him, in essence, to seek out and command as much power within the organization as he could grab.

Clark's first season in San Francisco was clearly a success. The Niners went 8–6 and they would have been at least two games better if special teams hadn't been disastrous. San Francisco kicker Steve Mike-Mayer went into an awful slump in the second half of the season, making less than 50 percent of his field-goal attempts in the final weeks. He also missed 4 of 30 extra-point attempts and that shoddy performance kept the Niners out of the playoffs.

But the promising start had no chance of continuing. After Clark was hired, the 49ers went through ownership changes as the widows of Vic and Tony Morabito sold the team in 1977 to an outsider from Ohio. The Morabito widows and their advisers had come to the conclusion that the dramatic upturn in NFL salaries would keep them from competing and that it was time to get out of the football business.

Enter the DeBartolo family.

Ed DeBartolo was the founder and owner of the DeBartolo Corporation in Youngstown, Ohio. DeBartolo really had very little interest in the team or making the decisions that had to be made. But what he did want to do was buy his 30-year-old son Eddie DeBartolo Jr. a toy that he could own—and keep him from being involved the main portion of the family business, which included real estate, construction, mall development, and gambling interests.

The younger DeBartolo had enjoyed a life of privilege and nothing changed when he was thrust into the public eye as an NFL owner. He chose to remain in Youngstown instead of San Francisco, a move that did not sit well with San Franciscans, who had a great deal of pride in their city. If given a chance to live in San Francisco or anywhere else in the world, most fans couldn't understand why another choice would be necessary.

DeBartolo seized control of the franchise and he had to hire his own point man to run the team. He chose a controversial general manager in Joe Thomas—who had worked in Baltimore and Miami prior to coming to San Francisco—a power-hungry megalomaniac with more than a bit of phoniness in him.

Thomas always liked to run the show and tried to show the rest of the world—scouts, coaches, and media—that he was always the smartest man in the room. While in Miami, the Dolphins' scouts knew he was a phony and they once made up a fictional player's name and put it on the blackboard in the room where they were seated. When Thomas came into the room he proceeded to give a detailed scouting report on the player, making up the facts as he went along. Everyone in the room—with the possible exception of Thomas himself—knew who the phony was.

Clark was in Miami at the time of the incident and he had no use for Thomas at all.

"If there was one man in the world that I would not have turned my future over to it was Joe Thomas," Clark said. "With Joe, you never knew what was going to happen. You might love a particular player but the next day find out that he's gone. I worked with Howard Schellenberger at Miami and saw how ho was treated by Joe Thomas. I wanted no part of that and there was no way I was going to go along with that."

Clark knew the 49ers were making a mistake and he tried to advise DeBartolo that bringing in Thomas would be a huge mistake. "I told them that they had to operate with class and dignity in this city—and that was not Joe Thomas," said Clark. "I told them that Thomas did not have that ability and that it would be disastrous. I went over it many times and I knew that I could not and would not work with the man."

DeBartolo tried to convince Clark to stay and coach the team, working with Thomas. But there was never any movement and never any indication from Clark that there was a reason to stay.

Clark was fired by DeBartolo with three years remaining on his contract. The DeBartolos promised to honor the deal, but the team would be run by Thomas.

DeBartolo knew the decision to fire Clark and hire Thomas was unpopular but he didn't care. "Joe Thomas was a friend of ours long before we ever got involved in the football business," DeBartolo said. "I let him know that if we ever got involved in football ownership we wanted him involved with us. We wanted Monte Clark to stay as head coach. However, we did not want him to run the personnel department. Even if it had not been Joe Thomas we would have made changes in that area and renegotiated Clark's deal."

The Thomas era became known for one thing—incompetence.

Thomas hired Ken Meyer as head coach in 1977 and then fired Meyer after a 5–9 season. Pete McCulley and Fred O'Connor were the head coaches in 1978. The team went a miserable 2–14 and was one of the worst franchises in all of professional sports.

Thomas was probably even worse in the personnel area than he was at picking coaches. He released Jim Plunkett; the former Stanford great was picked up off waivers and went on to win two Super Bowl titles with the Raiders. He inexplicably traded five draft picks for a washed-up O.J. Simpson, who was no longer able to compete because of various knee ailments. Thomas's drafts were without merit. The worst of those was a Notre Dame tight end named Ken MacAfee, who was selected with the number seven overall pick. MacAfee was unable to catch a cold, let a lone a key pass in the NFL.

In addition to his incompetence on the field, Thomas alienated nearly everyone he came into contact with while conducting business with the 49ers. He disrespected long-time employees of the club, stuck his nose in the air when conducting business with the local government. He was rude and obnoxious with the media.

Call him the anti–George Bailey. Think of the protagonist of Frank Capra's classic movie *It's a Wonderful Life*. When Bailey was considering suicide as a result of his memory-challenged uncle's financial gaffe, he was given the gift of seeing what life would have been like if he had never existed. That allowed him to gain a clear view and change his mind.

If Thomas had had that opportunity, he would have seen that pro football in San Francisco would have been much better off without him and he'd have to choose another profession.

DeBartolo ended up firing Thomas, but only because the team had fallen so far. He would have kept the irascible Thomas just to show the media and the community who was boss, but there would have been no substance to that decision.

So, Thomas was fired...and Bill Walsh was brought in.

It was a move that would turn the 49ers into one of the best organizations in all of professional football.

Chapter 2
A Major
Rebuilding Project

"If you have to win a game or score a touchdown or win a championship, the only guy to get is Joe Montana."

—Randy Cross

Laying the Foundation

Bill Walsh's first years as head coach of the 49ers were challenging. When he inherited the team in 1979, it was a complete mess. San Francisco had been 5–9 and 2–14 in the two previous seasons. The team had little talent and couldn't have been more unimaginative. The offense lacked talent, but even if it had a few decent players the coaching staff wouldn't have had any idea how to deploy those players.

When Walsh came on the scene, the first thing he did was what he knew best—built a proficient offense. Walsh had learned from some of the great innovators in the game—Sid Gillman, Al Davis, and Paul Brown—and his own vision and creativity allowed him to come up with his own game plan for success.

Walsh had hoped that his 1979 team would be much better than the previous year's team. But during training camp, Walsh realized the weapons were not there for the Niners to be able to grind out victories. He was not discouraged. He wanted to see improvement even if the team continued to lose. He didn't buy into the philosophy that winning was everything. In 1979, his goal for the team was overall improvement. If his team played tougher, smarter, and was more competitive than it had been the previous year, he would be satisfied.

Walsh's on-field expertise was offense, but as head coach of the team he installed a new management system that would be tantamount to the team's success. While it ended up with Walsh making nearly every key decision, he was a consensus builder. He wanted the opinions of all the key people in his organization before he made a final judgment.

On the field, one of his most notable moves was to step up the organization in practice. Walsh allotted specific times for each drill. He put all his plays in at once and if the players didn't follow all the specifics right away, he still moved on to the next play. Many other coaches wouldn't put in a second play until his team understood the first play without fail.

His practices tended to be significantly shorter than that of

Stanford head coach Bill Walsh gets a lift from his team after the Cardinal defeated the Georgia Bulldogs 25–22 in the Bluebonnet Bowl game on January 1, 1978. He would take over as coach of the 49ers the following season.

other teams. He had his players spend more time in the film room and the classroom studying the playbook because he wanted his team to be mentally prepared. As the season progressed, his practices all but eliminated hitting because he wanted his players to be fresh.

Walsh also brought in a number of waiver-wire players for work-outs since his team was thin on talent. Most were easy to eliminate after a short drill session but he found a fine pass rusher in Dwaine "Pee Wee" Board and a solid defensive back in Dwight Hicks.

After his first year, Walsh went after as many quick and agile offensive linemen as he could find. He came to the conclusion that those players would be far more productive than the big 300-plus starting to take shape. If his key players stayed healthy, it had a chance to be formidable. But he knew that a major upgrade was needed on defense and Walsh addressed it in the 1981 draft.

In particular, Walsh wanted to upgrade the secondary. The Niners lacked defensive backs who could cover top-level receivers or tackle with authority and consistency. He had his eye on UCLA safety Kenny Easley and USC defensive back Ronnie Lott. Both were sharp, smart, and dynamic players who had rare charisma to go along with their game-breaking talent. In the end, Easley went to the Seahawks and Walsh picked Lott.

The 49ers also picked three other defensive backs, Carlton Williamson, Eric Wright, and Lynn Thomas. Williamson and Wright would become key contributors while Lott would turn out to be a Hall of Famer.

In addition to the rookie talent, Walsh also brought in veteran linebacker Jack "Hacksaw" Reynolds after the Los Angeles Rams released him. Reynolds was 34 when the Niners brought him and had slowed a step or two, but what he lacked in quickness he made up for in intensity and sure-handed tackling.

Walsh had high hopes for Reynolds to become a significant contributor as well as providing an upgrade on the defensive chemistry. It worked out even better than he had planned. The pieces were in place and the Niners were ready to make history. All they had to do now was play the game.

A Quarterback Named Montana

There's Joe Montana. And then there's everybody else.

At least that's the way 49er fans look at it when it comes to quarterback play. Those fans may be prejudiced and may not give Steve Young, Johnny Unitas, Dan Marino, or John Elway their due, but they just may be right about Montana.

Montana was the MVP in three of his four Super Bowls and led his team on "the Drive" in the other.

He possessed an almost mystical calmness in the midst of chaos, especially with the game on the line in the fourth quarter.

pounders that nearly every other team went after. He also wanted a quarterback who was athletic and could make good decisions on the field. Arm strength was not one of his top priorities.

The Niners' system required the quarterback to learn the responsibilities of each receiver on the field, and it was somewhat complicated because there were so many options. While it was somewhat intimidating at the start, Joe Montana and Steve Young grew to love it because there were so many potential receivers. "Any decent quarterback should be able to complete at least 60 percent of his passes in this system," Young said.

The key to the West Coast offense is the quarterback's confidence in where his receivers are going to be. There are no variations with the routes. The only time a receiver would alter his route is if protection breaks down and the quarterback has to scramble. Otherwise, Niner quarterbacks knew just where their receivers were going to be.

In Walsh's first year on the sidelines with the 49ers, Steve DeBerg was his quarterback. DeBerg was a smart, strong-armed quarterback who was excited to be in Walsh's system and had all the attributes needed to be successful—with the exception of quickness and foot speed.

The Niners immediately became a more interesting and exciting team than they had been in the two previous seasons, but not necessarily a better one. DeBerg completed 347 of 578 passes and gave the Niners' offense the capability it had been missing. The contrast between 1978 and '79 got 49er fans into their team once again. They had been among the most boring teams in recent memory, but in less than a year they were throwing the ball all over the lot.

However, Walsh was not enamored with DeBerg as his quarterback because he was too slow to get away from the pass rush. Instead of running out of trouble or throwing the ball away, DeBerg put the ball up for grabs way too often. He threw 21 interceptions and each one seemed to cause problems.

There was significant improvement during the start of the 1980 season when the Niners opened the season with three straight wins. However, Walsh was concerned after the third win because he had lost pass rusher Dwaine "Pee Wee" Board to a knee injury. The Niner defense still had a long way to go and the only thing that made it respectable was the ability to put pressure on the quarterback. Without that ability the Niners lost eight games in a row, including a 59–14 humiliation at the hands of the Cowboys.

The Niners pulled out of their funk at the end of the year and won three of their final five games. The most notable of those games was a Week 14 38–35 victory over the Saints. The Niners trailed 35–7 at halftime, but they pulled off a monster comeback.

The orchestrator of that comeback was a young quarterback named Joe Montana, who had been drafted in the third round out of Notre Dame in 1979.

Montana was average sized and his arm was decent, but he did not have impressive physical characteristics. What he did have was great football intelligence, confidence, and accuracy in his passing. The Niners' scouting department liked what they saw from Montana and so did several other voices that Montana respected. However, when it came to judging quarterbacks Walsh always relied on himself. He saw enough physical talent and the kind of charisma and overall attitude that would make Montana an outstanding leader for the team.

Going into the draft, Walsh's favorite quarterback was Phil Simms of Morehead (Kentucky) State, who was taken in the first round by the Giants. The Niners never had a shot at Simms because they had no first-round selection, having traded it to Buffalo for O.J. Simpson. Bringing one of the NFL's most exciting running backs back to his hometown team was a disastrous move by previous general manager Joe Thomas. Simpson had bad knees and nothing left in the tank and it was the beginning of the end for him. Of course, in years to come Simpson would have much greater problems off the field than he ever did on it.

In addition to Simms and Montana, Walsh also took a look at Clemson quarterback Steve Fuller. Walsh went to South Carolina to watch Fuller throw the ball and he was not impressed. But the receiver Fuller was throwing to caught Walsh's eye. Dwight Clark was big, athletic, had great leaping ability, and had excellent hands.

Walsh liked Montana quite a bit from what he had seen and in reports he had gotten from scouts and coaches. He even more impressed when he saw Montana work out in pe More than anything, Walsh was enamored with Montana's foot

"It comes down to a combination of athletic ability knowing what he's doing," Walsh explained. "He had very feet and set himself up in the pocket with ease. If the play b down, he moved decisively to either run or get rid of the bal knew how to do this when he came to us and we were ab work with him and build on this ability. Some quarterbacks learn how to do this during their career while others never get hang of it. Joe knew from the beginning and it remained one of greatest assets throughout his career."

Walsh developed Montana very carefully after selecting h He threw only 23 passes as a rookie—and did not have one in cepted. Walsh usually gave Montana an opportunity advantageous situations—when the Niners had the ball inside t red zone. Not only was this good for Montana's confidence, it w beneficial for the team.

"How many times do you see coaches turn to young quarte backs who are simply not prepared to play in the NFL?" Wals said. "It's bad for the team and it can be disastrous for the playe A young quarterback throws three or four interceptions early in his career and that game can stay with them. The doubt creeps into their minds and it never leaves."

By the midway point of the 1980 season, Walsh decided that Montana was ready to be the Niners' starter. DeBerg understood what was going on and that Montana was the team's quarterback of the future, but that didn't mean he liked it. DeBerg, who would eventually become one of the better quarterbacks in the league when he manned the position for the Kansas City Chiefs from 1988 through 1991, was one of the most competitive players in the league and was well respected by his teammates. The last thing Walsh wanted was a quarterback controversy, so he traded DeBerg to the Broncos.

By the end of the 1980 season, Walsh knew his offense was

Despite rather ordinary physical gifts, Joe Montana started displaying his great skills as soon as he put on his 49ers uniform. The 1981 season marked the beginning of his ascension into pro football royalty.

While others saw turmoil and danger after the snap, Montana saw order and opportunity. He was Joe Cool, the unflappable king of the comeback.

Montana was neither exceptionally fast nor tall, and he didn't have a bazooka for an arm. The man about whom his high school quarterbacks coach said "was born to be a quarterback" won by wits and grace, style and reaction. It was as if he saw the game in slow motion. Whether it was with Notre Dame or the 49ers, whether the game was played in an ice storm in Dallas or in the humidity of Miami, Montana was "the Man" in the fourth quarter.

"There have been, and will be, much better arms and legs and much better bodies on quarterbacks in the NFL," said former 49ers teammate Randy Cross. "But if you have to win a game or score a touchdown or win a championship, the only guy to get is Joe Montana."

Sports Illustrated titled a story on the fragile-looking quarterback "The Ultimate Winner." Montana won four Super Bowls in four appearances and became the only player to earn the Roman-numeral game's MVP three times (and the other contest was that game-winning drive).

In these four games, he put up Super numbers, completing 83 of 122 passes (68 percent) for 1,142 yards with 11 touchdowns and no interceptions. His quarterback rating was 127.8. (While nobody outside the Elias Sports Bureau knows how to compute this rating, or even what it means, it is known that 127.8 is a figure beyond that of mortal men.)

He made the throw on the play that became known as "the Catch." That's when a scrambling Montana, with three Cowboys closing in for the kill, lofted the ball into the end zone to Dwight Clark. The 6-yard touchdown pass—with 51 seconds left—gave the 49ers a 28–27 victory over Dallas for the 1981 NFC championship.

"At his best, when Joe was in sync he had an intuitive, instinctive nature rarely equaled by any athlete in any sport," said Bill Walsh, his San Francisco mentor and coach, about the two-time NFL MVP.

As a redshirt junior at Notre Dame in 1977, after sitting out the previous season because of a separated shoulder, Montana took the Irish to a national championship. In his career he led them to five improbable fourth-quarter comebacks (with deficits ranging from eight to 22 points).

The most dramatic comeback was his last collegiate game at the 1979 Cotton Bowl, when he fought hypothermia in the ice and wind in Dallas. After being fed bouillon during the second half to get his temperature back up to near normal, he led Notre Dame from a 34–12 deficit to a 35–34 victory in the final 7:37, throwing a perfect pass to Kris Haines for a touchdown with no time remaining.

"Joe was born to be a quarterback," said Jeff Petrucci, his high school quarterback coach. "You saw it in the midget leagues, in high school—the electricity in the huddle when he was in there. How many people are there in the world, three billion? And how many guys are there who can do what he can do? Him, maybe [Dan] Marino on a good day. Perhaps God had a hand in this thing."

Montana had a quick setup, nifty glide to the outside, and the ability to scramble under control—buying time, looking for a receiver underneath. And this was when he was still in high school.

Montana's roots are in western Pennsylvania, the cradle of quarterbacks. Marino, Johnny Unitas, Johnny Lujack, Joe Namath, George Blanda, Jim Kelly, and Terry Hanratty are from the area. All were tough, dedicated, hard workers, and competitive. "We had a no-nonsense, blue-collar background," Unitas said.

Montana was born in New Eagle on June 11, 1956, the only child of Joe Sr. and Theresa, and raised in nearby Monongahela. The family lived in a two-story frame house in a middle-class neighborhood and Joe Sr. helped his son get involved with sports.

Young Joe played baseball (three perfect games in the Little League) and basketball (he was offered a scholarship to North Carolina State), but after becoming a Parade All-American quarterback as a high school senior, he followed his idol, Hanratty, to Notre Dame.

At one time a seventh-string quarterback, he was still number three when the 1977 season started. But in the third game, with once-beaten Notre Dame losing 24–14 to Purdue, "the Comeback

Kid" came off the bench to throw for 154 yards and a touchdown in the final 11 minutes to lead the Irish to a 31–24 victory.

Coach Dan Devine finally saw the light and installed Montana as his starter. Notre Dame didn't lose again, and won the national title by defeating number one Texas 38–10 in the Cotton Bowl.

After capping his collegiate career with the comeback against Houston the following January, Montana was selected by the 49ers in the third round of the 1979 draft, the number 82 overall selection. Walsh brought him along slowly and it wasn't until late in his second season that Montana became the starter.

In 1981, the 6'2", 195-pound Montana was in complete control of Walsh's West Coast offense, and he led he 49ers to a 13–3 record. They won the NFC title with "the Catch," and defeated Cincinnati 26–21 in the Super Bowl.

Returning to the Super Bowl three years later against the Miami Dolphins, Montana upstaged Marino, who had thrown for a record 48 touchdowns. He passed for 331 yards and three touchdowns in a 38–16 San Francisco rout.

Montana suffered a ruptured disc throwing a pass in the 1986 opener and underwent a two-hour back surgery. Doctors told him it might be better for his health if he gave up football. Two months later he was back, throwing three touchdown passes to Jerry Rice. But the season ended the way it had begun—in pain. Montana was knocked out of a 49–3 playoff loss to the Giants when nose guard Jim Burt, a future teammate, buried his helmet under Montana's chin.

Three years later Montana had another Super Bowl ring. During a late scoring drive, Joe Cool smoothly hit eight of nine passes, with his 10-yard strike to John Taylor giving the 49ers a 20–16 victory in Miami.

The next season, under George Seifert, Montana took the 49ers to a 14–2 record. San Francisco won its postseason games by 28, 27, and 45 points (55–10 over Denver in the Super Bowl) and Montana completed 78 percent of his passes for 800 yards, 11 touchdowns (five against Denver), and no interceptions.

An elbow injury caused Montana to miss 1991 and further complications caused him to sit out until the final game of 1992.

With Steve Young entrenched at quarterback, Montana was traded to Kansas City in 1993. He led the Chiefs into the playoffs in his two seasons with them before deciding that, at age 38, he was finally weary of the game.

Few quarterbacks and coaches have had the partnership that Joe Montana had with Bill Walsh. "Joe had some advantages," Walsh told the *San Francisco Chronicle*. "He was in a situation where there wasn't much pressure on him because nobody expected him to win." (The 49ers had their second straight 2–14 season in Montana's rookie year and were 6–10 in his second.)

"By that time," said Walsh, "I had had a lot of experience in working with young quarterbacks. I'd done it with Virgil Carter, Greg Cook, and Kenny Anderson at Cincinnati, with Dan Fouts in San Diego, and with Guy Benjamin and Steve Dils at Stanford. So I had a definite plan in mind."

At the time, Steve DeBerg was quarterbacking for the 49ers, and he was a solid veteran who understood Walsh's system with a strong enough arm to cause problems for opponents. However, DeBerg had the mobility of a statue and when he was under pressure he often threw the ball into coverage. The resulting interceptions were a huge problem for Walsh and he knew he had to find a quarterback with more mobility who knew what to do when pressured.

Enter Montana. Walsh took him under his wing. More than practicing just passing and understanding how to get the ball to NFL-caliber receivers, Walsh wanted him to understand that he would not just be throwing the ball under the pristine conditions of perfect protection. Instead, Walsh wanted Montana to get used to rolling out and throwing on the run. It was a technique he would use throughout his career.

In the 1980 season, Montana started to emerge as an NFL force. Montana and DeBerg often alternated starts and Montana grew in stature each time he lined up under center. He served notice on the league that he would be a force to reckon with during a December 7, 1980, game with the Saints at Candlestick Park.

The Saints were absolutely miserable in 1980: they went

1–15 and their fans took to wearing paper bags over their heads and calling themselves the "Aints." But on this particular day, New Orleans was rolling in all phases of the game. Archie Manning was on fire, the running game was rolling, and the defense had tied up the Niner offense. The Aints were laughing as they ran off the field at halftime with a 35–7 lead.

The humiliation in the 49er locker room was palpable. Not only were the 49ers getting pounded in every phase of the game by one of the most miserable teams in NFL history, the results were getting to Walsh. He was feeling good about the progress his team had made throughout his second season, but this game was causing him to question himself, his coaching ability, and his future. If his team was about to get humiliated by the 1980 Saints, Walsh wondered how he could ever turn the team around.

Just as panic and dismay were about to set in, Montana asserted himself and led the 49ers on a comeback. In the third quarter, Montana scored on 1-yard run and then threw a 71-yard TD pass to Dwight Clark. They were still down by two touchdowns, but there was life on the sidelines.

In the fourth quarter, Montana threw a 14-yard TD pass to Freddie Solomon, and then the team completed the comeback when Lenvil Elliott scored on a 7-yard run to tie the score at 35–35. Finally, Ray Wersching booted a 36-yard field goal to give the 49ers the victory. The 38–35 win marked the greatest regular-season comeback of all time.

"That was really Joe's breakout game," Walsh told the *Chronicle*. "That gave him the confidence he could do the job."

Walsh went from the doldrums of impending doom to humiliation to the high of victory. He knew that Montana was the primary reason for the comeback and that he was capable of making magical things happen when he lined up under center.

Walsh knew it was time to hand the job to Montana and that meant trading DeBerg, who was quite popular among his teammates and had quite a bit of charisma.

In 1981, the 49ers became Montana's team. They went from a young group with potential to the start of a dynasty.

Montana's Top Eight Niner Moments

1. Super Bowl XIX versus the Miami Dolphins following the 1984 season: Even though the game was played at Stanford Stadium and it was practically a home game for the Niners, most of the attention was on Dolphins quarterback Dan Marino. Marino threw 48 touchdown passes and passed for 5,084 yards, both league records at the time. He got the pregame attention. Montana was almost ignored. No complaints from Montana, who was much happier performing on the field than he was talking about it.

Montana was on top of his game as he completed 24 of 35 passes for 331 yards and three touchdowns. He rushed five times for 59 yards and one touchdown. The 49ers sacked Marino four times, intercepted him twice, held Miami to a single first-quarter touchdown, and won the game 38–16.

"You don't mind being overlooked that much, but sometimes it seemed they forgot there were two teams in the game," Montana said. "It got to all of us after a while."

2. "The Drive" in Super Bowl XXIII following the 1988 season: The 49ers trailed the Cincinnati Bengals 16–13 when they got the ball at their own 8-yard line with 3:10 remaining in the game. This was the essence of Montana's cool. At one point in the drive, Montana was actually hyperventilating and having trouble catching his breath. Nonetheless, he took the 49ers 92 yards in 11 plays, throwing a 10-yard pass to John Taylor for the winning touchdown with 34 seconds to go.

3. The stretch from late 1988 to late 1990: During 37 games, Montana compiled a 34–3 record as a starter, completed 66.9 percent of his passes, averaged 8.71 yards per attempt and 252.2 yards per game, threw 74 touchdown passes and 21 interceptions, and won two Super Bowls. It is the phase of his career that guaranteed him a spot in the Hall of Fame.

4. Comeback at Philadelphia: In 1989, under coach Buddy Ryan, the Eagles had a fearsome defense. They sacked Montana eight times, but he kept getting up. He wound up throwing five touchdown passes, four of them in the fourth quarter, to rally the 49ers to a 38–28 victory.

This game would not have the glory of any of Montana's Super Bowl wins, but it is the game that stands out to him. The Eagles defense was at its best with Reggie White, Jerome Brown, Seth Joyner, and Clyde Simmons. Nearly any other quarterback would have been taken out of the game in an effort to save him for the rest of the season. Montana refused to come out.

"I always look back on that Philadelphia game," Montana said. "It was pure get punched in the mouth, get back up. Get punched in the mouth, get back up. Because of the way they played, we knew we were going to have another opportunity. It was a tough, physical match. Everyone was proud to come out of there with a win. That's the one for me I think about more than others."

5. His final Super Bowl: The 49ers' most lopsided championship victory was the 55–10 rout of Denver in the Super Bowl following the 1989 season. Montana completed 22 of 29 passes for 297 yards and a then-record five touchdowns. He probably could have thrown three more TD passes had he been so inclined.

6. Rally to win the division title: In a Monday night game against the Rams in Anaheim in 1989, the 49ers twice fell behind by 17 points. Montana, playing with bruised ribs, brought the 49ers from behind to win, 30–27, clinching the NFC West title. He completed 30 of 42 passes for 458 yards, a team record at the time including a 96-yard TD pass to John Taylor.

7. "The Catch" and the first title in the 1981 NFC Championship Game: With 51 seconds remaining in the game, Montana threw a 6-yard touchdown pass to Dwight Clark to lift the 49ers to a 28–27 victory that put them into the Super Bowl for the first time.

8. Biggest NFL comeback ever (at the time): In 1980, the 49ers trailed New Orleans 35–7 at halftime. The Saints had 20 first downs at the half, tho 10oro two. The Saints were 0–13 at the time. Montana drove the 49ers to four second-half touchdowns, and they won in overtime 38–35.

Chapter 3
The Keys to a Devastating Defense

The only way you can do anything is with passion.... Passion for playing, passion for living, passion for breathing."

—Ronnie Lott

The Legend of Ronnie Lott

At the end of the 1985 season in a game against the Cowboys, Ronnie Lott, then one of the premier defensive players in the NFL, mangled his left pinky in a brutal collision with running back Timmy Newsome. Bone fragments and parts of Lott's finger lay somewhere in the turf. Lott came out of the game briefly—a game his team won to gain a wild-card berth in the NFC playoffs. He bore the agony of his dismembered digit in the manner of all top guns and terminators of sports. Enduring the pain was a requirement—but what Lott went through and still remained in the lineup is the stuff of legends.

The next week, Lott had his fingers taped so he could play—in a loss to the Giants. Over that winter he remained in excruciating pain. He faced the next season with an awful choice: a complicated and delicate operation in which bone and skin grafting and the placement of pins in his hand might restore full use of his hand—or he could have the top of his finger amputated. Choice number one meant missing playing time and risking reinjury. Choice number two meant missing the top of his digit but being ready for battle. Most football fans know how this came out. Lott chose to have the top of his finger chopped off and then went on to his third Pro Bowl season with the 49ers, leading the team to yet another playoff appearance.

Ronnie Lott: the 49ers' Hall of Fame safety, a player who, more than most gained a reputation over a spectacular 14-year career for top-of-the-line intelligence (or seven yards behind the line) to go along with all that reckless intent. In a 1994 survey by the Sporting News, NFL coaches were asked to name a player who was the best candidate to become a head coach. Eight out of 20 placed Lott first on their list.

Lott has done as much as anyone to feed the myth that he is a psychopath in shoulder pads. He began his career in 1981 with the 49ers when the team was just another wind current in Candlestick Park. Over the next 10 seasons, he earned seven Pro Bowl selections and four Super Bowl rings. Because of his

Ronnie Lott always brought his viciousness with him on the football field. He knocked the ball away from Dolphin receiver Mark Clayton in Super Bowl XIX with a punishing hit that stunned the receiver.

unflagging and inspiring leadership, the 49ers became one of the strongest teams of the modern era. He switched around in the defensive backfield from cornerback to strong safety to free safety and, unbelievably, retained all-star status at each position. But above all he gained a reputation for his passion for the game and his equally fervent willingness to cajole teammates, and even staff and coaches, to go the extra mile.

Lott advertised his ferocious approach to the game in the 1991 book, *Total Impact*. In it he described his way of hitting as "driving through" a player he was tackling rather than merely bringing him down. He was known for the way he not only stopped opponents but seemed to dismember them in the process. Though he was a defensive back, an elegant greyhound, he hit more like a Greyhound bus. He was Lawrence Taylor and Mike Singletary and Reggie White—but playing where he did, he shouldn't have been.

Over the years, there have been as many stories of "Lott shots" as there are of atrocities in the supermarket tabloids. Former Redskins wideout Art Monk remembers what it felt like to be on the receiving end of a Lott shot. It was September 10, 1984. 'Skins and Niners. Monk took a ball on a deep slant and never saw Lott coming. Lott hit him full force in the back.

"Most guys would just hit you," says Monk. "But there's something about Ronnie…it's a different feeling."

Though he never let Lott know it, that hit, Monk says, "Pretty much messed me up for the rest of my career."

Another memorable and well-reported hit occurred in the '89 Super Bowl victory over the Bengals. Cincinnati running back Ickey Woods was picking up big chunks of yardage early in the game. After one long carry, Lott came to the sideline and told his teammates he would put a stop to it. San Francisco defensive coordinator Ray Rhodes recalls that Lott went out and knocked the will right out of the running back with one massive shot.

"It just knocked Ickey's spark right out of him," Rhodes says. "The game turned right then because Ickey just didn't run with the same authority after that."

True to the bulletproof reputation he had earned over the years, Lott even found a name for the way he hit people. "Woo-lick," he called it (as in wildly screaming "Woo" at the precise moment of collision). "Let me put my perception of hard hits into simpler terms," Lott said. "If you think you want to play in the NFL, and you want to find out if you can handle being hit by Ronnie Lott, here's what you do. Grab a football, throw it in the air, and before you can catch it, have your best friend belt you with a baseball bat. No shoulder pads. No helmet. Just you, your best friend, and the biggest Louisville Slugger you can find. That's what it feels like to be hit by me."

Former Niners stud offensive lineman and current broadcaster Randy Cross laughed at Lott's description. He practiced against Lott throughout his career. "It's funny to hear him say that, but that's exactly what it was like," Cross said. "Sure there have been bigger guys who deliver the hit but nobody throws himself at a player with as much ferocity as Ronnie."

Lott's game did not begin and end with the amputated finger or those bone-rattling hits. For all the blood on the turf, Lott was then—and always will be—one of the brainiest as well as one of the most dedicated players to wear the uniform. The best analogy to Lott's way of playing would be to Ted Williams's hitting. Or Jack Nicholson's acting.

"The only way you can do anything is with passion," Lott says. "Passion for playing, passion for living, passion for breathing. The essence of greatness, whether it's Mozart or Michael Jordan or [Microsoft founder] Bill Gates, is that they have an internal passion that cannot be denied, and they exemplify it through their perfection."

So how did Lott reach his level of dominance and leadership? Long hours, hard work, clean living, martial arts, and hours of study explain quite a bit. But then again, many other players who work out like demons and never break curfew couldn't bust a grape.

Lott's passion was as much in the planning as it was in the doing. The backdrop of the plan was always perfection and he came closer to reaching it than most players. His ability to set goals for himself and carry through started as a child. His father was a career military man, someone Lott says he wanted to emulate.

"My dad served our country through two wars," Lott says. "He was there in the Korean War and in Vietnam, although I don't think he served in combat. My dad in his uniform…I was always kind of proud of him, I wanted to be like him."

But he wasn't simply starstruck. His father and mother were real influences in his life. "My parents could have been disciplinarians only, but they weren't; they were much more than that," Lott says. He says his father especially made him see both sides of an issue, never forcing him to simply decide in terms of right and wrong. "Most kids are taught 'right, right, right,'" Lott says. "They are never taught why something is wrong. My dad was able to teach me that. He was able to teach me that something is right because something else is really wrong. He would always make me understand why something is wrong."

Being creative—as he learned from his father—meant, in sports, that there were no limitations, he was able to be as free as his imagination and his ability took him. "When I played as a kid, there were no limitations, I never had the sense, 'You have to do it this way and only this way,'" Lott says. "At home I used to love practicing by myself. You know, most kids never do that. I loved it. I was constantly throwing a ball up in the air and catching it; I'd imagine myself running for a touchdown or making a great play, whatever came to mind. Same thing when I was shooting baskets or even reading about great players. I'd imagine I was them."

Lott's father was also something of a basketball player—and basketball was Ronnie's earliest of passions. "I grew up watching and loving the Celtics, those old Bill Russell teams," Lott says. "I used to watch how they played, how committed they were, you saw them giving every second, you saw that they were committed to winning, you saw that they were committed to each other."

As he grew, basketball remained his favorite sport. He referred to himself as a basketball junkie. But then his basketball dreams led him to places that would enable him to be a very different kind of football player.

"I was a point guard in basketball, that was my love," Lott

says. "Drive for the hoop, right into the middle of everything and then get that assist, find someone who was open in the middle of all the traffic."

Lott devised peripheral vision exercises for himself. In school he sat still at his desk, staring straight ahead, the model of attentiveness. Whatever was coming at him from the front of the classroom, the real lesson he was absorbing was that he could see to either side of him: someone moving a paper, turning a head, raising a hand.

Nothing of what he did was ever merely technical. The Redskins, the Celtics, all of his individual sports heroes epitomized passion, doing it perfectly. "They used to call the Redskins the 'Over-the-Hill Gang,' and I loved that because they were always rising to new heights. There was a guy on the team, Pat Fischer, he played corner for 10 seasons. He was 5'9" and 170 pounds, and you always thought to yourself, 'How has this guy survived?' And the answer," Lott says, "was that he had to be that committed, he had to have that kind of passion."

Lott's father eventually moved the family to Rialto, California, a suburb an hour and a half from Los Angeles. Ronnie became a three-letter star for Eisenhower High and by his senior year was swatting away offers for college scholarships, nearly all in football. Eventually he chose Southern California, where he became a consensus All-American in his junior year. ("It was only at that point that I actually seriously thought I was going to have a pro career," Lott says. "Till then I was preparing to follow in my dad's footsteps, I would have had a career in the military.")

At USC, Lott had the good fortune of working with defensive coordinator Don Lindsey and coach John Robinson, who taught far more than fundamentals and college rah-rah. "Coach Lindsey always used to say there are two things you can control on a football field—your eyes and your feet," Lott says. "That sounds simple, but it isn't. I was taught then how to understand a football game—and I was a sponge. I'd look at the slightest variations in the way guys lined up or held themselves and I'd start to understand what was going to happen. I was taught that it's not film so much as understanding the rhythm of a game, its complexion. Teams will attack you differently when they're ahead or behind or how much they're behind or ahead."

What made Lott special as a defender is not really the violence of his game but the way he sees the field. His way of seeing allows him to make the plays he does, to go all out, to drive through a player rather than merely at him. Like a great point guard threading his way between flailing bodies, Lott acquired an ability to see almost in slow motion. When he describes how he makes a play, he makes it sound like it happens frame by frame, as though he is the most judicious kind of film editor in a cutting room.

"To break a play down, you almost have to see it in slow motion," Lott says. "It happens all the time. If someone's coming to block you and there's a running back behind him, you have to be able to decipher how to take on that block as well as how to get to the ball carrier. The process always varies depending on how they're coming at you, all kinds of things go into the decisions you have to make. One time you can see a guy's just a little off-balance, another time you pick up that he's running a block a little more inside—these are all minute things, barely perceptible, but from which you have to make split-second decisions. Well, you absolutely have to be able to make that split second slow [down] because if it's speeded up, you just don't make the play. You slow down the process, even though people in the stands or at home watching on TV think it's all happening in a blur."

Lott's view of the game is akin to Newton's view of gravity or DaVinci's take on art.

Even though he never saw him play, Jackie Robinson became a huge influence on Lott's life. "I can just picture in my mind what he had to go through then," Lott says. "How he had to say to himself all the time, 'Hey, I can do it.'

"And he had to be so tunnel-visioned, so focused that nothing distracted him from what he had to do; he saw it all in front of him so clearly that he could not only handle it but could even thrive and excel under all that pressure just to survive."

At the end of his career with the Jets, Lott knew he didn't have the physical capabilities he showed with the 49ers. He played the game more cerebrally in order to make up for what time had taken away. He also spent extra time conditioning, working with Ben Parks to get him prepared. Parks put him through a grueling, nearly spirit-breaking regimen that had as much to do with conditioning Lott's mind as his body.

"He saved my career; he got me stronger, faster," Lott says. "He got me strong in my mind because instead of sad he got me to go out there joyful. Instead of sitting around sulking about why I had been let go, I got myself focused again, where I'd go out and play and give everything I've got."

Lott was nowhere near the physical player at the end of his career that he was in the early part. Not that any of his opponents would have noticed. Lott still hit with the same ferocity, but he felt it nearly as much as opposing running backs and receivers. Those hits just took more out of him than they had years ago.

All of which was little comfort for those on the receiving end of Lott's signature hits. He was named to the league's 75-year anniversary team in 1994 and when the league names its all-century team in 2019, chances are he will be on that roster as well.

Hardy Brown—Setting the Hard-Hitting Tone

The San Francisco 49ers dominated the NFL throughout the 1980s and into the 1990s. They became one of the greatest franchises the game has seen, and they did it with a combination of skill, speed, intelligence, and innovation.

Game planning against Bill Walsh was almost impossible because he was simply more advanced in his strategy than 99 percent of the coaches that he would go up against. Joe Montana was more talented and accurate than 99 percent of the other quarterbacks in the league and the same held for Jerry Rice and Dwight Clark at the wide receiver position.

The Niners were widely admired for their talent. However, when it came to physical intimidation, most opponents didn't give the thought much consideration.

Players like Ronnie Lott, Dan Bunz, Keena Turner, Mike Walter, Matt Millen, and Charles Haley made sure perception was not reality. While the Niners' skill on offense was the key to their explosive ways, it was backed up by a defense that combined toughness and intelligence.

Physical play may not have been the lead item on the championship 49ers résumé, but a turn of the clock back to the physical 1950s shows that the Niners were one of the most punishing teams in the league. The 49ers were a hard-fighting and competitive team throughout the decade and often contended for the NFL's Western Conference title but were never able to get by the Detroit Lions, L.A. Rams, Chicago Bears, or Baltimore Colts.

However, a battle with the 49ers was almost a sure predecessor to a long engagement with the trainer. Opposing defensive players had to deal with powerful running back John Henry Johnson and opposing offensive players had to contend with a one-man wrecking crew at linebacker named Hardy Brown.

The 1950s were a decade when nearly every team had an intimidating player who could snuff the fight out of opponents. Players like Chicago's Ed Sprinkle, Baltimore's Art Donovan, Detroit's Joe Schmidt, and the Giants' Sam Huff were known for their ability to knock a player out with one shot.

None of them had anything on Brown. He had a knack for hitting players with his shoulder—and shattering them. In those days of the single-bar helmet, Brown would take his shoulder and level it at an opponent's cheekbone, nose, or jaw.

In the opening game of the 1953 season, Brown's shoulder nearly rubbed out Philadelphia Eagle running back Toy Ledbetter.

"It was early in the game and I was carrying on a sweep to the right," Ledbetter said. "I knew all about Brown and how he liked to play, so I always kept my eye on him. But on this particular play I lost sight of him. I cut to the inside and thought I was about to make some yardage. The next thing I knew I was on the ground and I was looking for my head. He came out of nowhere and hit me with his shoulder."

The shot broke Ledbetter's cheek. Eagle physician Dr. Tom Dow said it was the worst facial fracture he had ever seen—and not just on the football field.

How Brown created such mayhem was a mystery. He was 6' and 193 pounds—small for his position, even by the standards of the 1950s. Bears coach George Halas figured Brown had added something illegal to his equipment and had the officials check his shoulder pads. They found nothing.

Brown played college football at Tulsa, where he was a teammate of future Hall of Famer Jim Finks. He was a violent player in those days, even in practice. Finks used to tell a story about the Tulsa coaches using Brown on offense in the backfield in order to get the Tulsa defense game ready. He'd line up at fullback to get the left defensive end and at halfback to get the right defensive end. He did so well that he was used on both offense and defense in games as well. Finks described Brown as "intelligent, warm, and shy," nothing like the smoldering demon he was on the field.

He started his pro career with the Brooklyn Dodgers and the Chicago Rockets of the All-American Football Conference. The Washington Redskins cut him after eight games, then he signed with the Baltimore Colts. In one of his first games with Baltimore, he led with his shoulder and broke running back Joe Scott's nose. The Giants tried to take revenge on him by going after him on the next kickoff, but Brown just laughed.

The Colts folded after the 1950 season—a new version of that team would rise in 1953—and Brown went on to find a permanent home in San Francisco. Every hit was designed to be his signature blow and in one 1951 victory over the Cardinals, Brown broke six noses.

He was especially dangerous on special teams, where he could run downfield and smash opponents in an indiscriminate matter before he tackled the ball carrier. Former Lions linebacker Carl Brettschneider remembers that Brown was not above using the officials for cover as he ran behind them on his way downfield, launching his shoulder into the upper body and face of the opponent awaiting him. "He broke more jaws than any player I ever saw," Brettschneider said. "He never had any remorse either."

No, feeling sorry that he injured another player was never one of Brown's traits. Former Giants lineman Tex Coulter was one of Brown's childhood friends and he didn't think it was his intention to injure anyone intentionally. "I think Hardy just had a certain style," Coulter said. "He just had that power in his shoulder and he enjoyed using it. When you stick someone like that, it's an absolutely beautiful feeling. Hardy wanted to have that feeling again and again."

He would go on to finish his pro career with the Denver Broncos in 1960, the first year of the American Football League. However, it was with the 49ers that he made his mark as one of the hardest hitters the game has ever known.

Finesse? Brown never even knew the word.

Fred Dean, Pash-Rush Master

The focus is almost always on the quarterback.

That's the way it is in the NFL. Put a successful quarterback on a good team and championship dreams start to flower.

But a good quarterback—or even a great one—is just one piece of the puzzle.

A running game to handle short-yardage and red-zone situations and help bleed the clock in the fourth quarter. A devastating pass rush may be the second most important factor besides the quarterback.

At the start of the 1981 season, Bill Walsh knew his team needed help in both of those areas. The need for a big-play pass rusher was paramount if the Niners were going to climb the ladder. The semblance of a great passing game was there with Joe Montana and Dwight Clark, and rookies Ronnie Lott and Carlton Williamson gave the defense a new identity.

But the move that probably had the biggest impact on the season was the acquisition of Fred Dean from the Chargers. Bill Walsh was more than a bit surprised when he discovered that the

Fred Dean (74) and his teammates harassed Miami Dophins quarterback Dan Marino all day long in Super Bowl XIX. The 49ers won, 38–16.

Chargers were willing to move their best pass rusher. Sure, they had an abundance of players who could bring pressure in Gary "Big Hands" Johnson and Louie "Big Foot" Kelcher, but Dean was the best among them.

A generation or so ago, Dean was just a bit undersized at 240 pounds, but he had lightning quickness and more than enough strength to handle a 285-pound offensive tackle. Dean could run the 40 in 4.47 and that allowed him to just obliterate bigger, slower offensive tackles. But what made him so special is that he could take those offensive tackles and toss them aside if he wanted to. Nothing flukish there, because Dean was naturally strong. "I never lifted a weight in my life," Dean said. "I had farm-boy strength. I baled hay. I hauled logs. I ate good and I did not go to the gym."

Dean was acquired early in the season from the Chargers for

a second-round draft pick in 1983 and the Chargers also had the option of exchanging first-round picks that year. It turned out to be a monstrous steal for the 49ers, and it was a move that had to be made if the 49ers wanted to be taken seriously in the NFL.

Dean got to the 49ers in time for their Week 6 meeting with the Cowboys in Candlestick Park. Dallas was the standard bearer in the NFC and the 49er coaching staff knew that a meeting with Tom Landry and the Cowboys would be a good measuring stick.

A close win would have left the Niners fans in an ecstatic state, but there would be no such thing. The 49ers took charge early and blew out the Cowboys 45–14. Dean had two sacks and helped force a third. He was an immediate impact player.

Two weeks later, the Rams came to San Francisco with a mountain of confidence. They had never lost to the 49ers at Candlestick, having won 10 consecutive games there. Dean's presence was probably the key reason San Francisco was finally able to defend its home field against the Rams in a 20–17 victory. He had 4.5 sacks against Ram quarterback Pat Haden and was a factor all over the field.

Offensive tackle Keith Fahnhorst was amazed that the Chargers would let Dean get away, even if they had other talented pass rushers. "Defensive ends like Fred Dean are extremely rare," Fahnhorst said. "I don't think there's anybody like him. When I played against him as a rookie in the preseason [1975], I thought I would have an easy time because he was only 230 pounds. Instead, when they snapped the ball he went by me so quick that I didn't even see him."

While pass rushers with speed are much more versatile than they were in the early 1980s, the Niners found a way to use Dean all over the field. When he wasn't rushing the passer, he was dropping into coverage or moving from side to side.

Just as important as his on-field skills, Dean brought a fire and a passion that had been missing from the front seven. Dean wanted to make plays but he also wanted to leave his imprint on those who tried to block him. He played with a determination to punish. With an attitude that was similar to Dick Butkus and Deacon Jones, and one that would be matched by the Giants' Lawrence Taylor, Dean had the ability to make opponents question their career choice.

And he did it with old-school style. Trash-talking and finger pointing were starting to become popular in the early 1980s, but none of that was Dean. Before the snap of the ball Dean showed all the emotion of an office worker. But once the ball was snapped it was as if 100,000 volts of electricity were set loose inside him.

"I watched him in the huddle," Lott said. "He was always totally calm. But I've never seen a pass rusher like that in my life. He had this knack for getting off the ball quickly and moving with speed. And then when he took somebody on he had overpowering strength."

Walsh knew that great pass rushers earn their money in the fourth quarter. "The other team may have the lead, but in the NFL it was about putting the game away with one more drive or even one more first down," Walsh said. "If you have that dominating pass rusher, they can't make that first down or that key drive. You get the ball back and you have your opportunity. That's what Dean did for us."

Dean would finish the regular season with 12 sacks. The Niners would fulfill their early-season promise by winning the NFC Championship in memorable fashion when Montana hit Clark with the famous pitch and catch. A Super Bowl title against the Bengals would follow.

At the time, it was the Niners' offense that was thought to be the difference. It was a good offense and Montana would make a case for being the best quarterback of all time. But that 1981 team made the jump up the NFL ladder because of its defense.

The offense had been solid during the 1980 season, but the improvement of the defense the following year allowed the Niners to play at their own pace. The offense did not have to score 40-plus points every game. Thanks to Dean up front and Lott in the secondary, the Niners had a defense that complemented the offense.

That's how Walsh had envisioned his team when he took the job in 1979. Two years later he had built a championship team.

Dean was the last piece of the puzzle and he may have been the most important part.

Chapter 4
The 49ers Capture Greatness

"He threw up a floater and the only thing I could think of was a wounded duck, I didn't think there was any way in the world that anyone would catch it."

—Dallas defender Charlie Waters, describing "The Catch"

Dwight Clark's Miracle Catch

It is a play that has been diagnosed, analyzed, lionized, and turned into legend.

There has been much debate about Dwight Clark's catch of Joe Montana's pass on the back line of the end zone in the NFC Championship Game on January 10, 1982. But that one play—devised by Bill Walsh, executed by Montana, and finished by Clark—propelled the 49ers into a run of excellence resulting in five Super Bowl championships.

That play has become part of the NFL's highlight film—not just for the 49ers but for the league itself. It is shown alongside other legendary clips, like Alan Ameche crashing into the end zone for the Colts in the 1958 NFL Championship Game in Yankee Stadium against the Giants. Bart Starr following Jerry Kramer into the end zone against the Cowboys in the Ice Bowl. Lynn Swann leaping over the top of the Dallas defense in Super Bowl X. Giants wideout David Tyree's over-the-head catch of Eli Manning's miraculous escape and pass in the late stages of the Giants' shocking Super Bowl XLII win over the Patriots.

Clark's catch belongs with those great plays. Whether Clark is deserving of legendary status for the play is debatable—Montana made a perfect throw while buying time and fading backward—but it gave the Niners the momentum and confidence to become one of the greatest teams of all time.

Let's go back to that January afternoon. The Cowboys had long been the villains as far as 49ers fans were concerned. In three consecutive postseason appearances from 1970 to 1972, the Cowboys defeated the Niners to end their season.

While Walsh's 49ers had pounded the Cowboys during the regular season, pessimistic Niners fans were not convinced. Beating the hated Cowboys in the regular season was one thing, getting past them with all the money on the table was quite another.

It was back-and-forth throughout the game but the Cowboys asserted themselves in the second half. They had a 27–21 lead with 58 seconds left.

Dwight Clark leaps high to gather in a Joe Montana pass that tied the game late in the fourth quarter on January 10, 1982 against the Dallas Cowboys. The extra point gave the Niners a 28–27 win and a berth in the Super Bowl.

The Niners had the ball on a third-and-three play on the Co
6-yard line. During a timeout, Walsh and Montana discussed t
uation and Walsh decided on a play called Sprint Right Optio

Montana rolled to his right in order to have the longest a
of time possible to search for options. He was looking for Fr
Solomon in the middle of the end zone or Clark in the corne

As Montana sprinted to his right, Cowboy defensive er
"Too Tall" Jones had Montana in his sights. Joe had to avoid
first and then find an open receiver. It seemed like an impo:
task because Jones was 6'9" and had tremendous reach
extended his hands upward to obstruct the back who was
ing Montana's view. In addition to the obstruction that
provided, Montana was approaching the sidelines. He
running out of time and room to operate. He took one last
and thrust himself into the air. It appeared Montana had crea
positive play because he was not going to be sacked. But a to
down? No way. At least not at first glance.

But Clark was working the back line of the end zone ar
broke free just as the ball was at its apex. He leaped for the
and stayed in the air as the ball appeared to be just out o
reach. However, Clark stayed in the air and caught the ball
his fingertips.

The rest was up to gravity. It brought Clark down in the
zone with the ball firmly in his grip.

The touchdown gave the 49ers a 28–27 lead, but the Cov
still had enough time to get in position to attempt a game-wi
field goal. With Danny White behind the center, nobody do
that the Cowboys had the ability to do just that. But White fur
the ball and the Niners recovered to hold on for the win.

Walsh and Montana felt no pressure on the third-dowi
because they had another down to work with.

"I told Joe that if he did not see anything or that if there w
much pressure he should just simply throw the ball away,"
recalled. "It was third down and we would have another play a
as we didn't turn it over. As far as I was concerned, a sack
have been nearly as bad. It's one thing to make a play from the

line but it's quite another to do it from 20-plus yards away.

"I knew Joe was not going to make a mistake. He was either going to make the throw or throw it away. I had as much confidence in him at that moment as I had in any player. I wasn't sure that we would get everything we wanted on that play but I felt extremely confident that Joe wouldn't turn the ball over or take a loss."

Montana explained that having an extra down to work with was his security blanket. "We had plenty of momentum and we were confident," Montana said. "We had moved the ball down the field against this team and we had a chance to win. We sensed that they were the ones on their heels and facing pressure.

"I wanted to make a play but if I didn't make it on third down we would have another chance on fourth. I was looking for Freddie and he wasn't open. I just took my chances that Dwight would be there. I knew he could go up and get it. I didn't want the ball intercepted.

"I never saw him make that catch but I heard the reaction of the crowd and I knew we had scored."

The 28–27 victory propelled the Niners into their first Super Bowl. "The Catch" is not only a highlight-film play that defines NFL history, it also serves as the moment when the 49ers changed their own legacy. Prior to the catch, the 49ers were a Charlie Brown/*Peanuts* kind of team. *Good grief, what's going to go wrong next?*

But when Clark climbed the ladder and came down with the ball, it was a 180-degree reversal. The Niners would go on to win five Super Bowls in a 14-year span—an achievement no other team has come close to approaching.

1981 Running Game

The talking heads on television often talk about the tendency of coaches. For example, when Bill Parcells was coaching it was widely thought that he was a conservative coach who liked to drive the ball down his opponent's throat with the running game. In reality, Parcells

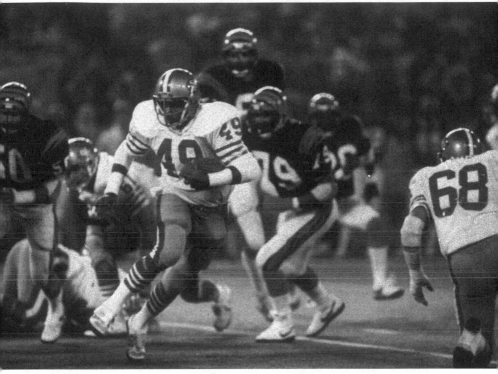

Earl Cooper, one of many 49ers running backs during the 1981 season, runs through a hole in the Bengals defense on January 24, 1982, in Super Bowl XVI at the Pontiac Silverdome in Michigan. San Francisco defeated Cincinnati, 26–21.

was a counterpuncher who passed when opponents thought he would run and ran when opponents thought he would pass.

Parcells used all the weapons on the field, including his tight end.

Bill Walsh was much the same. In the NFL the secret to long-term success is versatility. His version of the West Coast offense was largely perceived as a passing offense and he utilized the talents of Joe Montana, Steve Young, and a cadre of great receivers extremely well. But his use of the running game was also very effective. Especially during the 1981 season, when the Niners climbed the NFL ladder and became Super Bowl champions. Amazingly, they did it with a motley crew of running backs who were long on heart and short in every other measurable area.

The Cowboy Perspective

The Cowboys were not as confident headed into the NFC Championship Game as might have been expected from "America's Team." Tom Landry's team was aging and near the end of its halcyon days.

Veteran defensive back Charlie Waters and linebacker D.D. Lewis got their first shock when they pulled up to Candlestick Park's players' entrance in a limo. At the same time, 49ers linebacker Jeff "Hacksaw" Reynolds was arriving in a taxi.

Waters was elegantly dressed in a suit, but Reynolds got out of the cab in full uniform—including spikes and eye black.

"What a contrast," Waters said. "I'm in a suit and this guy has all his gear on. We made eye contact and he said, 'Bring it on.' It was clear that he was ready."

The conditions at Candlestick were awful. The turf was soft and muddy and it was in such bad shape that the NFL didn't even attempt to resod the field, figuring it was a lost cause. The grounds crew used some water-absorbing pellets to dry out the field and then painted the bare spots green so the field would look better on television.

While the Cowboys were never comfortable they still played a great game. They had the lead late in the fourth quarter and felt no discomfort when the 49ers took over at their own 11-yard line with the length of the field to go in order to take the lead. Joe Montana was directing the comeback attempt, but he was not yet a legend. He was a mere mortal at that point in his career.

But that was about to change. Rather than challenge the Cowboys with risky deep passes, the Cowboys utilized the short passing game along with some well-timed runs to move the ball down the field. However, the Cowboys thought they had the ability to keep the Niners from scoring and take the game when they came down to the final minute.

On the fateful play, Waters had an excellent view of Jones coming after Montana and the quarterback drifting farther away from the line of scrimmage and the end zone.

"He threw up a floater and the only thing I could think of was a *wounded duck*," Waters explained. "I didn't think there was any way in the world that anyone would catch it. But then that [Dwight] Clark went up and got it. It looked like he had jumped off of a trampoline.

It changed everything for that team and it ended my career. They took something away from us that should have been ours."

That's how Waters ended his career and it remains a painful memory. "I wanted to go out with a win in the Super Bowl," Waters said. "We had it and they took it away from us. That game clearly sent the 49ers up and got them going in the right direction. It was just as bad for us and it would be a long time before the Cowboys were a good team again."

Ricky Patton, Lenvil Elliott, Johnny Davis, Earl Cooper, Paul Hofer, and Bill Ring never had any chance to make it into the Pro Football Hall of Fame in Canton other than by purchasing a ticket. But that unfabulous fivesome somehow managed to give the 49ers a credible ground game throughout that season—and that gave Montana a chance to play his game.

Nobody understood the importance of that more than Walsh. He wanted his teams to display balance on the offensive end. The star power may have been with the quarterback and wide receivers, but the ability to make key third downs on the ground, make effective plays in the red zone, and, most important, keep defenses honest and allow the 49ers to keep the offensive options open.

"What is the key to offensive football?" asked former Eagles quarterback and current ESPN analyst Ron Jaworski. "It's having balance and not being predictable. Your primary choice may be moving the ball through the air, and that's probably the way that most effective offenses get most of their production from. To do that, you need to have a viable ground game. Today's defenses are too strong, too tough, and too smart to get defeated by a one-dimensional attack. It's about keeping the defense honest and not allowing them to only focus on what you do best. You have to be efficient and proficient at the things you do second best, third best, and fourth best. You do all those things well and then you can do what you do best when the game is on the line. Bill Walsh was a master at preparing his team to be effective in a number of areas—not just the short passing game that is associated with the West Coast offense."

During the 1981 season, the Niners rushed for 1,941 yards on 560 attempts. That works out to 3.5 yards per carry, far below their opponents' mark of 4.1 yards per carry. However, the Niners had 17 rushing touchdowns compared to just 10 for their opponents.

The running game showed up big in the postseason, including the famed drive against the Cowboys in the NFC Championship Game. When the Cowboys came out in a prevent defense designed to make it tough for Montana to go downfield, it left short passes available as well as opportunities to make things happen with the ground game. While none of the 49ers running backs scared opponents, Walsh chose to go with Elliott, who barely had a chance to play in the regular season because he was coming off a knee injury and subsequent surgery. But Walsh knew that Elliott had talent because the two had been together in Cincinnati in 1973.

Elliott had been fairly explosive in his years with Cincinnati and Walsh thought he was reliable. Elliott was in the backfield as the drive began and he rewarded the decision by running for 11 and 7 yards on the first two plays of the drive. Another run—a reverse to Freddie Solomon—gained 14 yards. The three running plays set the Cowboys back on their heels and the 49ers were quickly in Dallas territory. They found themselves with a first-and-10 situation at the Dallas 13 with 1:15 remaining. The play that everyone remembers—Dwight Clark's leaping catch on the back line of the end zone—put the Niners in the Super Bowl. But the running game allowed the 49ers to get downfield quickly and gave them the opportunity to make the big play.

The running game in the Super Bowl is one of the most overlooked aspects of the 49ers' win. They ran for 127 yards, and the ability to move the chains with the ground game paid huge dividends. They had 40 running attempts (compared to 24 by the Bengals). Patton had 17 carries for 55 yards, and while they didn't have a run longer than Earl Cooper's 14-yarder, the ground game kept the Bengals off balance throughout.

Walsh was triumphant and he called the win "the greatest moment of my life."

He thought his team was clearly a bunch of overachievers,

especially his underwhelming group of running backs. "This is a group of men who do not have great talent," he said. "But they do have the inspiration. They proved that every week."

Two years later the Niners would bring in a big-name running back in Wendell Tyler and draft Roger Craig. But a group of no-names did pretty well when the 1981 season—the pivotal year in the franchise's history—was on the line.

Beginning of a Giant Rivalry

Great champions earn that title because of their achievements. The 49ers have won five Super Bowl titles; only the Pittsburgh Steelers and Dallas Cowboys can match that total.

While the two Super Bowl wins over Cincinnati were memorable and close games, the triumphs over the Dolphins, Broncos, and Chargers were one-sided routs. From the mid-1980s through the late 1990s, the NFC was the dominant conference. The 49ers basically won their championships when they beat the top NFC opponents in the playoffs.

The 49ers' most significant rival has been the Dallas Cowboys. It took a victory over "America's Team," culminated by Joe Montana's pass to Dwight Clark in the corner of the end zone late in the fourth quarter, to get the Niners to their first Super Bowl. That play is not only symbolic of the franchise's sudden climb up the NFL ladder, but is also considered one of the most memorable moments in sports history.

As much as the 49ers and Cowboys have defined each other during the 1980s and 1990s, San Francisco also had its memorable moments against the Redskins, Bears, and Giants.

While the Bears had the same kind of image and persona as the 49ers, Mike Ditka almost always came out second best in his matchups with Bill Walsh. After the Redskins beat the 49ers 24–21 in the 1983 NFC Championship, the 49ers would go on to dominate the series, winning nine of the next 10 meetings, including two in the postseason.

But the Giants–49ers games had some special characteristics. Both teams came into prominence in the early 1980s. San Francisco was a bit more accomplished and skilled, while New York won with its brutish strength.

The clash in styles led to a series of memorable games. Neither team was intimidated by the other and that lack of fear led to even more big moments.

The 49ers and Giants captured five Super Bowls in the '80s and met four times in the playoffs during the decade-long rivalry. Not surprisingly, the winner of three of those four playoff games went on to win the Super Bowl (San Francisco in 1981 and 1984, and New York in 1986). While it was a series that featured some of the greatest players in history—Joe Montana, Jerry Rice, and Lawrence Taylor—the coaching staffs were even more impressive.

The rivalry was typically marked by a battle of wits between Bill Walsh and Bill Parcells—the decade's greatest offensive mind versus the decade's greatest defensive mind. The two men couldn't have been more different, with Parcells cutting an abrasive, emotional figure while Walsh played the role of the intellectual. In many ways, it was the '80s version of Belichick versus Dungy: two men held in the highest esteem, but for vastly different reasons.

The assistants under Parcells and Walsh also built impressive careers after cutting their teeth in the rivalry. The games featured a bevy of bright minds who would go on to distinguish themselves after Parcells and Walsh moved on. Among those coaches: Bill Belichick, Mike Holmgren, George Seifert, Tom Coughlin, Romeo Crennel, and Charlie Weis.

The 49ers would win their first Super Bowl title following the 1981 season, and that was the same year the Giants would return to the postseason after an 18-year absence. New York made the playoffs on the last game of the season, beating the Cowboys 13–10 in overtime. That game set off a wellspring of emotion in the locker room and among long-suffering Giants fans. The following week the Giants scored two touchdowns in the first minute of their wild-card meeting with the Eagles and managed to hang on for a 27–21 road win.

There was very little left in the tank for their cross-country trip to San Francisco. The Niners were healthy and rested and simply had too many offensive weapons for New York. Prior to the game, the talk among the New York media was that the 49ers wouldn't be able to cope with a team that had New York's back-alley toughness, but in truth it was New York's inability to handle the 49ers' precise and well-developed offense that allowed San Francisco to come away with a 38–24 victory.

Parcells would eventually become the team's head coach, but at that time Ray Perkins was in charge and Parcells was the team's defensive coordinator. The loss to the 49ers was disappointing for New York, but it also had some very positive moments. The Giants tied the game early on a 72-yard TD pass from Scott Brunner to Earnest Gray and later Brunner had another long scoring pass to Johnny Perkins. That touchdown brought New York to within 24–17, but Ronnie Lott ended matters with an interception return for a touchdown.

The teams would split postseason meetings following the 1984 and 1985 seasons. San Francisco would beat the Giants 21–10 in the 1984 divisional playoffs before the Giants would get a bit of revenge the following year in a 17–3 victory.

While the 49ers would go on to win Super Bowl titles following their two divisional playoff wins over New York, the physical Giants got treated like wounded bullies when they played the Chicago Bears in the divisional playoffs. Chicago punched New York repeatedly, registering a 21–0 victory, and that game showed the Giants that they had to bring their game up to another level when the money was on the table.

The 1986 season proved to be New York's best. They dominated the NFC with a 14–2 record and were ready for a peak performance when Joe Montana brought his team to Giants Stadium for a divisional playoff game. Playing on the road was perhaps the 49ers' greatest strength during their championship years, but it wasn't on this day.

The Giants had edged the 49ers in San Francisco 21–17 in a memorable come-from-behind win on Monday night. But there would be no comeback. It would be all Giants as the 49ers got served a full dose of humble pie.

The Giants got the scoring going with a 24-yard TD pass from Phil Simms to Mark Bavaro. Running back Joe Morris gave the Giant offense balance when he scored on a 45-yard run. After a Simms touchdown pass to Bobby Johnson, Hall of Famer Lawrence Taylor turned the lights out on the Niners when he picked off a Joe Montana pass and returned it 34 yards for a score. On the play, Giants nose tackle Jim Burt beat his block and crashed into Montana as he was about to deliver the ball. The result was a fluttering pass that Taylor easily picked off and a knockout shot for Burt.

The Giants offense continued to roll as Simms and Morris made big play after big play. The result was a 49–3 Giants win.

After the game, Walsh minced no words. "We got shattered out there by an outstanding team," said Walsh. "They played a perfect game. They destroyed our offense and they destroyed our defense. We went out there to compete and possibly come away with a close, tough win. Instead we were handled and dispatched."

That kind of brutal honesty would become a Walsh trademark. He would not hide from the brutal loss to the Giants; he would go back to it. Walsh could not stomach another humiliation and he made sure that his team would never take a beating like that again.

Chapter 5
Super Bowl Success

"I'll tell you, in that goal-line stand we were pretty much businesslike. Nobody made any speeches. We just concentrated on doing our jobs."

—Ronnie Lott

The Goal-Line Stand

It is fourth and a foot, Cincinnati trailing 20–7 late in the third quarter. All the Bengals need is 12 inches, and logic says Pete Johnson could get that much just falling down. There's a collision of helmets and shoulder pads. Johnson throws his body into the right side of the line.

The 49ers' Jack Reynolds, Ronnie Lott, and Dan Bunz sacrifice their own, which means the matchup is dead even. When the whistle blows, nose tackle Archie Reese is lying on top of the pile, his arms pumping toward the Silverdome ceiling in celebration. Pete Johnson's gain is measured in fractions. A stunned Bengals coach Forrest Gregg could only stand on the sidelines with his face buried in his hands.

"If I would've been betting on Pete Johnson making a foot," 49ers defensive coordinator Chuck Studley said later, "I would've bet everything I own that he'd make it."

The goal-line stand was just one more improbability in a giddy season for the 49ers, a team that didn't seem fit for drama such as this seven months before but was ready to be fitted for Super Bowl rings that night.

The team with three rookies, a second-year player in the secondary, and the no-name running backs had beaten the Bengals, 26–21, in Super Bowl XVI. And Bill Walsh, the coach of a 6–10 team the previous year, was being pulled away from a press conference to answer a telephone call from President Reagan. "You might tell Joe [Montana] and the rest of the fellas they really did win one for the Gipper," Reagan said.

"I think Joe was thinking about the Gipper when he won that one," Walsh replied. "Thank you very, very much."

The Bengals had pulled themselves out of a 20–0 hole—the largest halftime deficit in Super Bowl history—on a five-yard TD scramble by Ken Anderson in the first series of the third quarter. Two 49ers possessions had gained a grand total of minus-three yards and the Bengals were moving again. It was a fourth-and-one at the San Francisco 5, and the 49ers looked up just in time

Cincinnati Bengals quarterback Ken Anderson hands off to sledgehammer running back Pete Johnson (46), who is stopped at the goal line by the underrated San Francisco defense during third quarter action of Super Bowl XVI, on January 24, 1982.

to realize they had only 10 men on the field.

Linebacker Keena Turner was on the sidelines when Pete Johnson took the handoff and busted up the gut for two yards and a first down at the 3-yard line. "I didn't know I was supposed to be in there," said Turner, who swears he missed only one play, even though his coaches say it was two.

"Then a couple coaches started hollering at me. Then a couple players hollered. I think even the fans were hollering." Turner returned in time to see Johnson run behind left tackle Anthony Munoz for two more yards to the 1-yard line on first down. Here they were with three plays and less than a yard to go for a touchdown that figured to tighten the 49ers' windpipes even more. On second down, Johnson ran left again, but was stuffed by John

Harty and Jack Reynolds. On third down, Anderson threw a soft pass to running back Charles Alexander at the goal line, but backup linebacker Dan Bunz dropped him 12 inches short.

"I thought about going for the ball," said Bunz, who once had a bit part in *North Dallas 40*. "I figured it might be better to just stop the man instead of going for the ball."

It was as basic as you can get on fourth down. Pete Johnson weighs 250 and runs 350. The only surprise is that the Bengals didn't choose to run it behind Anthony Munoz.

"There wasn't much doubt about who was going to get the ball," said Jack Reynolds. "They had to give it to Pete. The guy is a Sherman tank. He's as big as a defensive lineman."

"I think that play depressed them," said Bunz. "I mean, how would you feel if you had Pete Johnson and you couldn't gain a foot?"

The Bengals had started the game in a similar depression and the goal-line stand brought back some not-so-distant memories. There was Kenny Anderson getting intercepted by safety Dwight Hicks at the Niners' 5-yard line just a heartbeat into the game, a play that followed 49ers return man "Famous" Amos Lawrence's fumble of the opening kickoff.

There was All-Pro wide receiver Cris Collinsworth fumbling at the Niners' 8-yard line in the second quarter when it was still a 7–0 game. Shortly after that, Joe Montana, who had scored on a one-yard dive in the first quarter, threw a 11-yard TD pass to running back Earl Cooper.

Montana, the game's MVP, moved the 49ers into field-goal range minutes later and Ray Wersching hit his first of four Super Bowl record—tying field goals—a 22-yarder that made it 17–0 with 15 seconds left in the half.

Then came a play that Bengal fans will never forget—even if they wish they could. Wersching squibbed the kickoff ("That was an accident," he later said) and Archie Griffin bobbled it just inside the 20. Then Bengals defensive back Ray Griffin tried to pick it up at the 10.

Wersching trotted downfield and kicked a 26-yard field goal with two seconds left to make it 20–0. The last time the city of Cincinnati felt this numb, it was 59 degrees below zero outside.

"Basically," said Bill Walsh, "our offense just swept them off their feet in the first half. I would say the turning point was that last field goal. I know we certainly appreciated the points."

If the Bengals were torched by the 49ers' beautifully designed passing offense in the first half, then they died a slow death at the brass-knuckled hands of the 49ers' defense in the second. The Bengals did manage to score on a four-yard pass from Anderson to tight end Dan Ross to make it 20–14 in the fourth quarter, but it came nine valuable minutes after the goal-line stand started.

Then the 49ers were forced to prove themselves one more time. They moved downfield for another Wersching field goal, this one a 40-yarder that made it 23–14 with 5:25 left in the game. Montana (14 of 22 for 157 yards) had been finding Dwight Clark and Freddie Solomon open all day, but the play that hurt the Bengals most on that drive was a 22-yard, third-down pass to rookie wide receiver Mike Wilson. Wilson was such an improbable hero that he made Dan Bunz look like Ted Hendricks.

The game was over when 49ers corner Eric Wright—another one of the adolescent All-Stars—intercepted an Anderson pass at the Bengals' 47 and returned it far enough for Wersching to kick a 23-yard field goal with 1:57 left. The Bengals would score again on a three-yard pass to Ross, who set a Super Bowl record with 11 catches, but it came too late to matter to anyone except the bettors and Ross's agent.

When it was over, the 49ers were the first team ever to win a Super Bowl without gaining more total yards than the loser. They already were the first team ever to get this far with so many question marks at the beginning of the season.

Teams aren't supposed to win a Super Bowl with three rookies in the secondary, and there were times in this game when the 49ers had four. You're not supposed to win when you do something like fumble the opening kickoff or when you find yourself playing a man short inside your own 10. And you're not supposed to be able to stop Pete Johnson from gaining a foot with the Super Bowl possibly on the line.

"I feel like a kid waiting on his first bike at Christmastime," said

Archie Reese. "He looks under the tree and there it is."

"There were a lot of hard times this season," said Ronnie Lott. "Like back in training camp when people were calling us clowns. But I figure we're kinda like a newborn baby. You just cuddle it, tease it, mold it until it grows up to what you want it to be. That's what this organization did with this team.

"We're kinda emotional. But I'll tell you, in that goal-line stand we were pretty much businesslike. Nobody made any speeches. We just concentrated on doing our jobs.

"It'll be one of those Super Bowl memories, the kind we've been watching all week in our hotel rooms. I got somebody back home taping the game for me. And you know what? I'm gonna replay that goal-line stand as soon as I get home. I'm gonna watch it the whole off-season."

Sealing the Deal

The 49ers defeated Cincinnati 26–21 in Super Bowl XVI. The architects of the win were head coach Bill Walsh and quarterback Joe Montana. Walsh came out with a sensational game plan and Montana executed it to near perfection as the Niners built a 20–0 halftime lead and managed to hang on in the second half.

Holding off the Bengals is now the stuff of legend, anchored by a defense that kept Cincinnati out of the end zone in the third quarter despite a first-and-goal situation from the 1-yard line. The goal-line stand became one of the Super Bowl's most memorable moments as well as a section in this book.

But even with the early scoring and the great play of under-rated players on defense, the Bengals had a chance to get the ball in the final seconds for an opportunity that could have produced victory. When Dan Ross caught a 3-yard TD pass from Ken Anderson with 16 seconds to go, the Bengals had climbed to within five points of the 49ers. Bengal head coach Forrest Gregg didn't even have to call for the onside kick. It was obvious that placekicker Jim Breech would try to work some magic with the kick and that his teammates would try to recover it so the Bengals could have two or three plays in an attempt to get into the end zone and give the Bengals the Super Bowl.

As obvious as it was for the Bengals to send out the onside kick team, it was just as clear that the 49ers would send out their hands team. That meant Dwight Clark would be right in the middle of the scrum. He would attempt to catch and secure the football, snuffing out all hope for the Bengals.

Clark was one of the best receivers in the league and had made perhaps *the* key play in 49ers history two weeks earlier when he made "the Catch" in the Candlestick Park end zone over Dallas cornerback Everson Walls and the Niners had beaten the Cowboys 28–27 in the NFC Championship Game.

Despite having made that play, Clark was anything but confident as he jogged out on the field. "All I could think about was that unfortunate onside kick against Dallas [in a 30–28 Cowboy divisional playoff win following the 1972 season] when they fumbled it," Clark said.

Former Niner Preston Riley had a chance to secure an onside kick that would have given the Niners a 28–23 victory over the Cowboys. However, Riley could not hold on to the ball and the Cowboys picked it up with 1:20 remaining in the game. Cowboys quarterback Roger Staubach took full advantage of that opportunity and drove Dallas to a 30–28 win. His 10-yard TD pass to Ron Sellers still burns in the memory of many 49ers fans.

"That's all I could think about as I ran across the field," Clark said. "Back then, the kickers didn't know how to kick down on it so it would slam into the turf and then bound 30 or 40 feet high. Instead, Breech kicked it and it bounced along the ground twice and it came right to me. I caught it, fell to the ground, and there was Ronnie Lott as my personal protector. I knew nobody was going to get to me. I looked at Ronnie and he started screaming, 'We're Super Bowl champs!'"

Clark picked himself up and flipped the ball to the official as he jogged back to the sidelines. "I regret that move," he said. "I only wish I would have held on to the football and kept it."

Behind the Scenes at Super Bowl XVI

That couldn't have been Bill Walsh in the Bell Captain's uniform could it?

Bill Walsh created the most enduring off-the-field image of Super Bowl XVI when he dressed as a bellhop and fetched luggage as 49ers players checked into their Michigan hotel.

It was an interesting moment—humorous, strange, and tension releasing.

It has since become part of Super Bowl lore.

But there were two other confidence builders before that game. Tight end Charle Young, who had been voted the 49ers' most inspirational player in 1981, strolled to the bulletin board in the locker room before the game and scrawled, "We are world champions." Young then delivered an impassioned speech, making sure his fresh-faced teammates understood the opportunity before them.

"I wanted to breathe life into our team," Young said. "I wanted guys to know we were going to win."

Rookie cornerback Ronnie Lott got the message. The other notable pregame scene was Lott playing Queen's "We Are the Champions" full blast on the boom box above his locker. Defensive end Jim Stuckey recalled several players "rocking out," as he put it.

Then the 49ers went out and validated their bravado. They beat Cincinnati 26–21 to complete their improbable march to the championship, only two years after a second consecutive 2–14 season.

Walsh orchestrated the rapid turnaround. His revolutionary West Coast offense helped the 49ers improve to 6–10 in 1980, and the cavalry arrived in '81. The 49ers drafted Lott, Eric Wright, and Carlton Williamson to join Dwight Hicks in the secondary, signed free-agent linebacker Jack "Hacksaw" Reynolds in June and traded for Fred Dean, a dominant pass rusher, on October 2.

Dean's arrival completed the transformation of San Francisco's defense, which became as instrumental in the title run as Joe Montana and the offense.

"The guy who truly made the difference was Fred Dean," Young said. "Until we got Fred, we were just another team."

Bill Walsh was dressed as a bellhop as he greeted Lawrence Pillers and the rest of the team at their suburban Detroit headquarters prior to Super Bowl XVI. Walsh flew in on another flight and was at the hotel in advance of the team.

The 49ers started the season 1–2, with road losses to Detroit and Atlanta. Offensive tackle Keith Fahnhorst was so discouraged after three games, given all the losing in previous years, he asked the 49ers to trade him. "That kinda tells you I didn't see it coming," he said.

Fahnhorst pointed to the October 11 victory over longtime nemesis Dallas as the launching pad. The 49ers clobbered the Cowboys, 45–14, at Candlestick Park (with Dean collecting three sacks in his San Francisco debut) and eventually won 12 of their last 13 regular-season games.

They had a nice mix of rising stars, such as Montana and Lott, and steely veterans, such as Reynolds and Young. It also helped that Walsh was a magnificent motivator.

"Coach Walsh was able to make people feel like they were the transmission and the motor, not just the taillight," running back Lenvil Elliott said.

That was evident in the postseason, when a variety of players contributed to the defeat of the Giants in the first round and then the Cowboys in a riveting NFC title game. Montana and Dwight Clark were not the only heroes of the Cowboys game: Elliott ripped off several big runs on the 49ers' last drive, Wright made a game-saving tackle, and Lawrence Pillers forced (and Stuckey recovered) Dallas's final fumble.

Then came the Super Bowl, when running back Earl Cooper scored one touchdown, the 49ers built a 20–0 halftime lead and the defense made its memorable goal-line stand in the third quarter.

"No one expected us to do what we did," Hicks said. "We all knew we were pretty damn good, but that didn't come out until after the year was over, the dust had cleared, and we sat on top of the league."

Super Bowl XIX—Marino Denied

The 49ers may never have been a better team than they were during the 1984 season. They reeled off 15 wins in the regular season and outclassed the Giants and Bears in the postseason before taking on the Dolphins in Stanford Stadium.

The game in Palo Alto, California, was basically a home game for the Niners, but it was the Dolphins who commanded the attention of the media. The meeting between the Niners and Dolphins had many storylines, but the one that most writers glommed onto was a quarterback matchup between Dan Marino and Joe Montana.

At the time, Montana was a great quarterback who was on the verge of becoming a legend. Marino was just finishing his second year in the league and it had been an eventful one. Marino became the first player ever to throw for 5,000 yards (5,084) in a season. He shattered the NFL record for touchdown passes in a season with 48, and his 362 completions and four 400-yard games also were league records. He led the league in pass attempts, average yards per attempt and efficiency rating. Entering the Super Bowl, he had passed for at least one touchdown in each of his last 22 games, including four in an eye-catching performance against Pittsburgh in the AFC Championship Games.

In addition to the numbers, his powerful arm along with a quick-as-a-hiccup release had given him a limitless future.

Since Marino and Montana were on the upside of their careers, many thought the two best quarterbacks in the league would have an opportunity to battle it out in several Super Bowls.

It didn't happen. The Dolphins had many good seasons with Marino, but they were never the all-around team that they needed to be in order to get back to the Super Bowl. He retired in 2000 with the regret that he had never won a championship. He could also take comfort in the fact that many longtime observers thought he was the top quarterback in the history of the game.

"He was the greatest competitor of all time and he had a great, great arm in which he had ultimate confidence," said Shula. "He played a few dozen games so breathtaking it was a privilege just to be there and he had career numbers in front of everyone. Dan was the best, the greatest quarterback of all time. But there's so much more to his rich life and you have to look at the whole picture."

Even with all of his achievements, it still hurts. His Hall of Fame numbers don't erase all the regret and pain: most pass attempts,

8,358; pass completions, 4,967 (records broken by Brett Favre in 2007); most yards passing, 61,361; most yards passing in a season, 5,084; touchdown passes, 420 (broken by Favre last season); touchdown passes in a season, 48 (broken by Peyton Manning in 2004 and Tom Brady in 2007); most games 400 yards or more passing, 13; most games 300 yards or more passing, 63.

Marino will admit that seeing Brett Favre win his Super Bowl title with the Packers over the Patriots in January 1997 was very tough to take.

"That was a tough one because I was still playing and it was late in my career and I still had this great desire to be there," Marino acknowledges. "I never used to go to the [Super Bowl] games. I'd go home and watch on TV but, for this one, a friend invited me and I went and it was weird. I figured I'd just leave in the second half and I did. I was always an optimistic player. Every year I thought we had a chance even though, realistically, we probably didn't because we weren't as good as nearly half the teams in the league. But I always felt, coming into the beginning of the season, 'This is going to be our year'. And season after season I became more focused on that goal because I wanted to know what it feels like and be in that situation and, you know, time was running out."

Winning a Super Bowl title became an obsession in his final years. "Obsessive to the point where I believed in my heart I was working hard enough to get there and our teams were working hard enough but not to the point where, if it didn't happen, I was going to allow it to ruin my life."

Despite all his success on the field and off of it, he finds himself looking back at the opportunity the Dolphins had in Super Bowl XIX. "I still wish we could play the game again [against the 49ers]," he accepts. "It was like it happened and it was over. We lost and I never had another opportunity to go back and play in the Super Bowl. I got close a few times but when I look back that's the one thing [missing] in my career. I felt every other experience possible as a professional athlete except winning the Super Bowl and knowing what it felt like when I came off the field to be a champion and be part of a championship team. That's the one thing. I had a great career and I have no regrets except not having that feeling. That was my second year, I was 23 years old and I felt, 'Damn, I'm going to be back here for sure'. Then it ends 15 years later and I didn't get back. But I felt I would definitely be back in the Super Bowl, sure. Without a doubt.

"We knew how good the 49ers were and that they would definitely get back to the Super Bowl. But they were in the NFC and we were in the AFC, so I felt we'd have that opportunity again to play in it. Nothing conspired against us, it's just a tough deal to get to the Super Bowl. The NFL is so competitive and a lot of things have to go right for you. You have to get with the right people, the coaching, you have to stay healthy, so many things. It's not being conspired against, it's more like being with the right team and having that opportunity. I'm not just talking about our team, I'm talking about being with the right group. I'm not saying we didn't have it because there were times when we were good enough and it's not like we weren't working for it every year. We worked our butts off and winning the Super Bowl was something I wanted to do. But it hasn't changed my life. If I had won, I'm not sure my life today would be any different."

But as mature as Marino's words are, you have to wonder whom he is trying to convince, himself or his listener.

Marino is as grounded as a former NFL star could be. He got the work ethic from his father, who worked the nightshift in the newspaper delivery business. Marino learnt early there are no short cuts to the top, that the best make it there for a reason. "The city of Pittsburgh and the neighborhood where I grew up had a huge impact on how I was as an athlete," he suggests. "I grew up in a competitive neighborhood, Parkview Avenue in Oakland, and the city of Pittsburgh and the people had a real impact on me.

"My dad passed on to me a love of sports. I played baseball as well as football and reached a pretty high level. The Kansas City Royals selected me and that was a real option, to play pro baseball, but I chose football at the age of 17 because college rules meant I had to make the choice."

Marino would love to have won a Super Bowl but he has long

since been able to put that into perspective. "There was a guy I was college roommates with, Tommy Flynn," he relates. "He was the high school quarterback for a team that went to the state championship when I was the big guy in Pittsburgh. He played defensive back for Green Bay, they released him, then the Giants picked him up and went on to win the Super Bowl. He blocked a punt in the final regular season game, won a Super Bowl ring, and played a special part. I never had that, but life goes on."

Chapter 6
Bill Walsh's Lasting Legacy

"I never should have left. I'm still disappointed in myself for not continuing. There's no telling how many Super Bowls we might have won."
                                    —Bill Walsh

Call Him the Genius

Bill Walsh earned the nickname "the Genius" during his tenure as 49ers head coach. What Walsh could do strategically was unmatched by any head coach of his era, including Hall of Famers Don Shula, Tom Landry, and Bill Parcells.

When he was hired in 1979 by the Niners, he took a downtrodden team and built one of the greatest teams in pro sports history. Walsh got his team to the top by using short, precisely timed passes to control the ball in what became known as the West Coast offense. He guided the team to three Super Bowl championships and six NFC West division titles in his 10 years as head coach.

It took more than an innovative offense for Walsh to become one of the most revered figures in Bay Area history—and we're not just talking about sports figures. With his white hair and professorial bearing, he conquered the pro football world with a combination of clever strategy and rugged defense. He was a thinking man's football coach—who studied and took cues from some of history's great military leaders. His manners seemed somewhat off-base to the football insiders who expected their head coaches to have a buzz cut, scream obscenities at their players, and try to dominate the opponent with the running game.

The 49ers had been wrecked by mismanagement and unwise personnel decisions prior to his arrival. Walsh, who had led Stanford to two bowl victories in two seasons as head coach, took a 49ers team that had finished 2–14 in 1978 and built a Super Bowl champion in three years. It was one of the most remarkable turnarounds in professional sports history.

His teams would win two more Super Bowls (following the 1984 and 1988 seasons) before he turned the team over to George Seifert, who directed the 49ers to two more championships (1989 and 1994). Walsh set the foundation for an unprecedented streak in the NFL of 16 consecutive seasons with at least 10 wins.

He had the ability to recognize and develop talent to its fullest. He was at his best when picking quarterbacks. He drafted Joe Montana in the third round in 1979 and acquired Steve Young, then a backup with the Tampa Bay Buccaneers, in 1987 for second- and fourth-round draft choices. Both were elected to the Pro Football Hall of Fame.

At his own Hall of Fame induction in Canton, Ohio, in 1993, Walsh revealed he nearly didn't make it to the end of his second season in San Francisco.

"In those first three years, we were trying to find the right formula," he said. "We went 2–14 that first year [1979]. The next year we won three and then lost eight in row. I looked out of the window for five hours on the plane ride home from Miami after the eighth straight loss, and I had concluded I wasn't going to make it. I was going to move into management."

He changed his mind and finished the season, a 6–10 year. The 49ers gave notice of things to come in a late-season game against the New Orleans Saints at Candlestick Park. Trailing 35–7 at half-time, they thundered back to win 38–35 in overtime. It was the biggest regular-season comeback in NFL history.

But the real magic was yet to come. After losing two of their first three games in 1981, the 49ers would win 15 of their next 16 in a methodical yet astonishing march. Behind Montana and wide receivers Dwight Clark and Freddie Solomon, and a defense led by linebacker Jack "Hacksaw" Reynolds, pass rushing whiz Fred Dean, and a secondary that started three rookies—Ronnie Lott, Eric Wright, and Carlton Williamson—they became the first NFL team in 34 years to go from the worst record to the best in just three seasons.

To do it, they had to shock the Dallas Cowboys 28–27 in the NFC Championship Game in January 1982. They won it on Montana's scrambling six-yard pass to a leaping Clark with 51 seconds left. The play, dubbed "the Catch," is the most celebrated moment in Bay Area sports history.

"That was a practiced play," Walsh said. "Now, we didn't expect three guys right down his throat. That was Joe who got the pass off in that situation, putting it where only Clark could come up with it."

Walsh showed his zany side two weeks later in Pontiac, Michigan. Arriving before the team, he borrowed a bellman's uniform at the hotel and collected the players' bags at the curb, even holding out his hand for tips. His players didn't immediately recognize him,

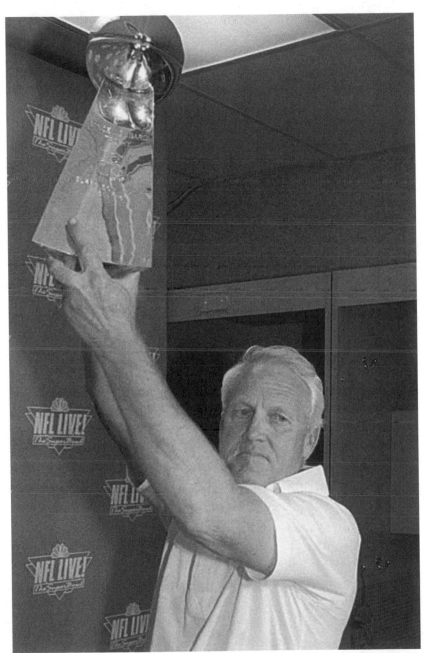

Bill Walsh raises the trophy after his team beat the Cincinnati Bengals 20–16 to win Super Bowl XXIII on January 22, 1989, in Miami. It would be the last game Walsh would ever walk the sideline as head coach of the Niners.

including Montana, who got into a brief tug-of-war with him when Walsh tried to grab his briefcase.

In Super Bowl XVI, the 49ers built a 20–0 lead but needed a memorable goal-line stand in the fourth quarter to hold off the Cincinnati Bengals and win 26–21.

Pro football in San Francisco would never be the same.

Walsh and his players were stunned by the reception they received when they returned to San Francisco. "There was a suggestion of a parade for us," Walsh said years later. "And I remember thinking that with the general fatigue, I was reluctant to put the players through something that might be just a few people waving handkerchiefs on the street corner."

A few people? Walsh was never more wrong. There were more than 500,000 people screaming, crying, and cheering as the 49ers were welcomed home with a parade down Market Street.

"It was just an overwhelming experience, the realization that millions and millions of people had been following us," Walsh said. "That's when I realized what an accomplishment, what a historic moment for the city, it was to win a professional championship."

The 1984 team was probably Walsh's finest, an 18–1 powerhouse with a record-setting offense and the league's stingiest defense. It pounded Dan Marino and the Miami Dolphins 38–16 in Super Bowl XIX at Stanford Stadium. The following spring, Walsh drafted a receiver from Mississippi Valley State named Jerry Rice, and the offense got even better.

A last-ditch catch by Rice on a pass from Montana stole a victory over the Bengals in 1987. The play was memorable not only because it won the game but because it prompted a bizarre reaction by the head coach: Walsh joyfully skipped off the field.

One of the most thrilling Super Bowls (XXIII) followed the 1988 season. Rice was voted the game's Most Valuable Player after making 11 catches for a Super Bowl–record 215 yards. But the 49ers needed a 92-yard drive engineered by Montana in the final minutes and a last-minute 10-yard TD pass from Montana to John Taylor to beat Cincinnati 20–16.

A few minutes later in the locker room, Walsh hugged his son

Craig and, to the surprise of others in the raucous celebration, burst into tears. A week later, he revealed why he was so emotional: he had decided he'd had enough earlier that season. He was stepping down. "This is the way most coaches would like to leave the game," he said.

Despite another Super Bowl title, Walsh did not enjoy the 1988 season. He bumped heads with owner Ed DeBartolo and his relationship with the media got testy. The Niners were only 6–5 through their first 11 games and did not look anything like a Super Bowl team. Clearly that last year was a strain on Walsh, who was often at odds with DeBartolo and the media. The team struggled to its 6–5 start that year, and Walsh later said his intensity was waning, partly because he was "weary of the daily press-sparring."

Walsh was getting tired of the scrutiny and started to feel the pressure of leading a great team. "You become the victim of your success. Everybody expects nothing but wins. They ignore that 27 other franchises have equal desires and opportunities, and that so-called parity gives winning teams tougher schedules and poorer positioning in the draft.

"Owners demand high production. Fans get to where they can't understand why you lost, even if the team makes the playoffs before bowing. And the media, they always want to know how you lost, who screwed up, why it wasn't done differently, and every detail about your personal life."

The decision to leave haunted Walsh and he later told the *San Jose Mercury News* that the team could really have reached the stratosphere. "I never should have left. I'm still disappointed in myself for not continuing. There's no telling how many Super Bowls we might have won."

Before the championship 1988 season, there were three straight years of first-round playoff defeats. Even though the 49ers compiled the NFL's best regular-season record in 1987, their playoff loss caused DeBartolo to strip Walsh of his title of team president. In the ensuing years Walsh and DeBartolo patched up their differences, and DeBartolo was Walsh's presenter at the Hall of Fame.

He was named the "Coach of the '80s" by the selection committee of the Hall of Fame. His impact on the NFL was evident in the number of his assistants who went on to head coaching jobs, including Seifert, Dennis Green, Mike Holmgren, Ray Rhodes, Sam Wyche, Bruce Coslet, Mike White, and Paul Hackett. Those coaches in turn spawned a host of other coaches, all imbued with Walsh's distinctive offensive schemes.

He was an expert in developing quarterbacks, including Ken Anderson, Virgil Carter, and Greg Cook with the Bengals, Dan Fouts with the San Diego Chargers, Guy Benjamin and Steve Dils at Stanford, and, of course, Montana and Young with the 49ers. He said he looked for resourcefulness, creativity, and passing accuracy in his quarterbacks; arm strength was far down the list.

He said that the West Coast offense started with the Cincinnati Bengals, where he was quarterbacks coach and offensive coordinator under coach Paul Brown from 1968 to 1975. Walsh borrowed from the principles of Sid Gillman, the legendary San Diego coach, and others.

"It was born of an expansion franchise that just didn't have near the talent to compete," he said. "That was probably the worst-stocked franchise in the history of the NFL.... The best possible way to compete would be a team that could make as many first downs as possible in a contest and control the football.

"We couldn't control the football with the run; teams were just too strong. So it had to be the forward pass, and obviously it had to be a high-percentage, short, controlled passing game. So through a series of formation-changing and timed passes—using all eligible receivers, especially the fullback—we were able to put together an offense and develop it over a period of time."

The West Coast offense meant the ball could be thrown on any down or distance. It meant having the quarterback get rid of the ball quickly to limit the risk of sacks or turnovers. It didn't mean ignoring the running game, but it could make up for a weak rushing attack. For example, the 49ers' leading rusher in their first championship year was Ricky Patton, who had just 543 yards.

"The old-line NFL people called it a nickel-and-dime offense," Walsh said in his book. "They, in a sense, had disregard and contempt for it, but whenever they played us, they had to deal with it."

He pioneered the idea of scripting a game's first 25 plays, a habit he started with the Bengals. At first it was just four plays, then six. When he went to the Chargers, it was 15, then 25. He refined the script at Stanford, and it later was a staple with the 49ers. The script was never a hard-and-fast list; he would stray from the list if the situation warranted, then return to it later.

"The whole thought behind 'scripting' was that we could make our decisions much more thoroughly and with more definition on Thursday or Friday than during a game, when all the tension, stress, and emotion can make it extremely difficult to think clearly," he wrote.

Practices under Walsh were not the bruising sessions they were under most other coaches. "We didn't beat guys up," he said. "It was practice. Practice so we could play our best in the game—and not leave it on the practice field. We tried to prioritize because there have been many situations in this game where teams have been flat. They had nothing in their emotional tank since they had been beaten up so badly in practice. If you think about it, that's just plain silly."

Walsh could rarely be heard screaming on the practice field. If a player made mistakes or hurt his team, Walsh would let him know. Not with epithets and a raised voice, but through straight-forward conversation and direct action, such as benching or getting rid of a player.

Again, Walsh took the path less traveled. It was a journey that left him high on the coaching pedestal, along with greats like Vince Lombardi and Don Shula. It is elite company, but Walsh showed he truly belonged.

Memories of Bill Walsh

"The essence of Bill Walsh was that he was an extraordinary teacher. If you gave him a blackboard and a piece of chalk, he would become a whirlwind of wisdom. He taught all of us not only about football but also about life and how it takes teamwork for any of us to succeed as individuals."

—NFL commissioner Roger Goodell

"I was sorry to learn about the passing of Coach Bill Walsh. He was an outstanding coach and was a special friend.

"He was a great competitor and was one of the most innovative coaches in the game. The offensive philosophy that he installed in those great 49er teams more than 25 years ago will remain his legacy and is still very much a part of the NFL to this day.

"My wife, Mary Anne, and I were very saddened when we heard the news and we know we join football fans around the country who feel a deep sense of loss. Our thoughts and prayers are with his wife, Geri, and their family."

—Former Miami coach Don Shula

"I was saddened by the news of the passing of Bill Walsh. He was one of our fiercest rivals. Bill was an innovative coach and we engaged in several memorable games in the '80's. Bill leaves a great legacy and an impressive coaching tree. He is one of the guys who made the NFL what it is."

—Former Giants, Patriots, Jets, and Cowboys coach Bill
Parcells

"Bill Walsh's legacy with the 49ers is well documented. The 49ers remained his team even after he left the organization. He dedicated his life to football, and all 49ers fans, current and past, are forever grateful.

"I will miss my weekly talks with Bill each Monday following our games. He was always so supportive and always offered some thoughts to help me in any way he could.

"He was not only an outstanding coach but a tremendous role model for every one associated with the 49ers and our fans.

"Although I never worked for Bill, I always considered him a mentor during my 21 years in the NFL. He not only made a legendary impact on the game of football, but he was also instrumental in issues such as diversity in the NFL and in developing player assistance programs."

—49ers head coach Mike Nolan

"There is not a player at the 49ers or a player in the NFL today that was not touched by the contributions of the legendary Bill Walsh. Without a doubt, Bill Walsh is clearly one of the greatest coaches in NFL history. His achievements during his 10 years as head coach of the San Francisco 49ers are virtually unparalleled in professional sports.

"While he will go down in history as one of the greatest and most innovative football minds of all time, we also will always ohorish the close connection we had between our families that developed over the past three decades of our lives. It is with great sadness that we offer our condolences and prayers to Geri and the Walsh family.

"Outside of his family and faith, there was nothing he loved more than the 49ers. Even after he left the organization he still kept up with the team and offered his support.

"Bill exemplified class, and all of us in sports should honor him by striving to perpetuate his standard of excellence."

—49ers owners John and Denise York

"Bill was blessed with one of the greatest gifts you can have, which is the ability to see the future potential of another human being."

—Hall of Fame quarterback Steve Young

"This is just a tremendous loss for all of us, especially to the Bay Area because of what he meant to the 49ers. For me personally, outside of my dad, he was probably the most influential person in my life. I am going to miss him."

—Hall of Fame quarterback Joe Montana, the player most closely linked to Walsh's tenure with the 49ers

"When you talk about a Hall of Fame coach, a guy who's won Super Bowls, for me just to have the opportunity to speak with him and be around him on an everyday basis when I was in San Francisco was definitely an honor."

—Cowboys and former 49ers receiver Terrell Owens

"He did a magnificent job. And we here on the West Coast have to wake up and realize that not everything happens at the Heisman, the Maxwell Award, and all these awards that are given back East to great contemporaries and see that we too, our culture, has developed people and certainly he represents the West Coast.

"When we were with him on Saturday, he told us that he had had enough. It was a great life."

—Al Davis

"It's not just how he prepared his teams and his attention to detail and his training camps that all of football is still emulating. As a minority coach, here is a guy who stood on a table and said, 'A door should be opened.' His impact is so far beyond football. He opened a door worldwide that made a better America, not just a better American football.

"There was a time where minority coaches did not have the opportunity to be exposed and did not have access to the meat and potato aspects of coaching and football executive positions. What Bill Walsh did was allow all those coaches to learn and then bring that knowledge back to their coaching staffs. He did a great, great service to all of us."

—University of Washington coach Tyrone Willingham, the first coach to participate in the minority coaches fellowship established by Walsh

"What really made Bill special is that he understood that the game was bigger than him. His genius was not centered around Xs and Os; it was centered around his ability to create a platform that made the game inclusive to others. He will forever be cemented with the likes of George Halas, Paul Brown, and Vince Lombardi as the best ever."

—Ronnie Lott, Hall of Fame defensive back who played for 49ers from 1981 to 1990

"He and [Al] Davis and Sid Gillman were way ahead of their time when it comes to the passing game. You knew he definitely was well ahead of everyone else."
—Hall of Fame cornerback Willie Brown, who played and coached against Walsh-led offenses

"If you want to look at what embodied Bill Walsh, it was Joe Montana. He didn't make any mistakes. He knew where everything was; he wasted very, very little of anything. He always took what was there and ultimately won."
—Detroit Lions president and CEO Matt Millen

"He was one of the most creative people in the sport. Everywhere he went he was a winner. He was one of those unusual people who could say, 'Here's a play, it's going to work, and here's what's going to happen.' That's one of the hardest things in football."
—Former Washington Redskins coach Joe Gibbs, who coached against Walsh from 1981 to 1988

"I played for him for one year, and I learned a lot. But more important was that he was so supportive of me and my career and African American coaches. It's one of those things that really touches you."
—Indianapolis Colts coach Tony Dungy

"Beyond being a great offensive coach, Bill mastered running an entire pro football organization. He figured out everything from the big picture down to the smallest detail and documented it in his book, Finding the Winning Edge, *which was groundbreaking. It remains easily the most comprehensive and best modern-day football book and is required reading for every coach."*
—New England Patriots coach Bill Belichick

"Bill Walsh was one of the greatest coaches in the history of this game. I am not sure that anyone has had as much influence on the way the game has been played over the past 25 years as Bill Walsh. His record on the field was matched only by his brilliance in developing other successful NFL and college coaches."
—New York Giants president John Mara

"The thing with Coach Walsh that I will take through the rest of my coaching career was his ability to understand talent, the ability to go out and find pieces [that were] exactly what he wanted."
—Minnesota Vikings receivers coach George Stewart, who coached wide receivers in San Francisco from 1996 to 2002

"When I first came into the league, he was the first guy I worked with.... He took a kid from Augustana College and made him into an NFL quarterback."
—Ken Anderson, Pittsburgh Steelers quarterbacks coach, who played under Walsh for five seasons in Cincinnati when Walsh was the Bengals' quarterback coach

"He was a very demanding head coach. His presence put pressure on you. I mean, when he walked out of that locker room, it was all about football, getting your minds right. But that's just the personality he had and the impact he had on a team."
—Tom Rathman, Oakland Raiders running backs coach and former 49er

"Bill was an innovator, a motivator, and ultimately one of the most dynamic coaches in NFL history. From my earliest days of involvement in the NFL, he was a friend who always had time to offer his counsel and advice. His leadership defined the 49ers as the team of the 1980s, and his legacy will be as one of the best we have ever seen."
—Jerry Jones, owner and general manager, Dallas Cowboys

"The thing he did is he really went about putting the game in players' hands, and saying, 'You got to make plays. I may throw you a five-yard slant, but I expect you to turn it into a 30-to-40-yard play,' and he knew how to get the ball in his players' hands."
—Houston Texans coach Gary Kubiak

"Bill's record speaks for itself. He was the top coach in the NFL during his time in San Francisco. During his eight years on our coaching staff, he brought imagination and ideas to the game. He was a tremendous part of our staff, and we were lucky to have him. He set a mark on the game that is admired by everyone, and he will be greatly missed."
—Cincinnati Bengals president Mike Brown

"Everyone who loves football will miss one of the game's great icons. He was an extraordinary mentor to so many coaches who are still in the game today. We all owe him greatly for his kindness and gifts."
—Southern California coach Pete Carroll

"From day one he molded my career and helped me out tremendously. When you talk about the things he would do for his coaches, not only did he show you the on-the-field part of the game, but off-the-field part of the game as far as scouting, dealing with player contracts, just all aspects of football."
—Ray Rhodes, assistant defensive
backs coach for the Houston Texans

"Coaches my age, we all studied Bill Walsh as we were coming up in this business. We talked to the people who worked with him to try to find out why he did what he did and how he went about his business. Intellectually, he just seemed to be way ahead of everybody else."
—New York Giants coach Tom Coughlin

"All of us who had the fortune to spend significant time with Bill and sought his willing guidance will surely cherish every moment spent with this very special man."
—Philadelphia Eagles chairman Jeffrey Lurie

"Great coaches are great teachers, people who enjoy teaching. It doesn't matter what level it was on. I don't care if he was teaching high school kids, quarterbacks, three-to-five-step drops, college kids, pro kids, he enjoyed it. He was very good at it, very smart. I guess the best way to describe it is he just had passion for everything he did. And that's one of the reasons he was so successful."
—Denver Broncos coach Mike Shanahan

"He had great vision on what the league was going to become and how to forge opportunities for players. What he did for that organization, the Super Bowls he won, is a testament to what kind of coach he was. But he was also a good man who gave guys an opportunity."
—Kansas City Chief coach Herm Edwards

"Very few of us will leave legacies like he left in this game. He brought professionalism to the sport from ownership all the way down to the security people at the front door of the building. He taught people to treat people with respect. What he wanted people to know is that everybody meant something."
—Tennessee Titans coach Jeff Fisher

The Finesse Team

During the 49ers glory years, they were used to swaggering into battle with confidence and swaggering out of the game with a victory.

But after winning their second Super Bowl following the 1984 season, they went through a three-year period that was dominated by the Bears, Giants, and Redskins. But in 1988, the 49ers came all the way back and won their third Super Bowl title. It was one that was almost completely unexpected. They had a 10–6 record and won the NFC West over the Rams and Saints (also 10–6) based on having the best head-to-head record.

However, few thought the Niners would get past both the Vikings and Bears. Minnesota had thumped San Francisco 36–24 the previous season and featured a marauding defensive tackle in Keith Millard who could rip apart any offense. If they got past the Vikings, they would have to go to Chicago and beat the Bears in the middle of January.

The Vikings proved to be no problem as the Niners dispatched them 34–9. Still, that left a trip to Chicago in nearly arctic conditions.

At the time, the Bears were thought to thrive in those kind of conditions. Players bragged that they loved to play in winter conditions and dubbed it "Bear weather." The assessment had some chops because Mike Ditka's team had won its last 12 games at temperatures of 32 or below.

On this day, the windchill was minus-26 degrees. The "quiche eaters and wine drinkers" from San Francisco would be reduced to tears in a matter of moments. At least that's how Chicagoans saw the game.

Never mind that Bears defensive tackle Steve McMichael came out in pregame warmups wearing shirt sleeves. He was joined by outside linebacker Otis Wilson. These two "Monsters" were seemingly oblivious to the weather. When they were joined by placekicker Kevin Butler going out on the field without any protection it was all over. The Bears won in a rout.

Except somebody forgot to give that message to the 49ers. "Finesse" players like Joe Montana, Jerry Rice, and John Taylor led the Niners to an easy 28–3 win. By the midpoint of the second quarter the 49ers had control of the game and their grip never eased.

Especially notable was the domination of the 49ers front line against Chicago's previously dominating front four. Guards Jesse Sapolu and Guy McIntyre handled defensive tackles Dan Hampton and McMichael with eases.

Both men had been prepped for the battle by going up against Millard a week earlier. "That was the key," Sapolu said. "Yeah we had to go up against Hampton and McMichael and they are very tough.

But the week before we had to go up against Millard. That's an incredibly tough assignment. When you have to play against Millard — that's war. You get through that and you are ready for anything."

Hampton was a Hall of Famer for the legendary Bear defense and McMichael was nearly as good.

Oh, yes, a couple of players named Jerry Rice and Joe Montana also had a little something to do with the win. Rice caught two TD passes in the first half and the cold did not bother the Mississippi native who ran twice as fast as any of the Bears defenders. Montana whistled his passes to Rice, Taylor, and John Frank as if it were a summer day in Pasadena. He finished with three TDs.

The Niners overcame those obstacles and won a date with the Bengals in Miami for Super Bowl XXIII. Pushed to the limit by the Bengals, they came through with a memorable last second drive and won their third Super Bowl.

As usual, the heroes were Montana and Rice, but it was the underappreciated play of the offensive line that got the job done when the game was on the line.

The Game Plan

Much was made of Bill Walsh's decision to script his team's first 10–15 plays during his tenure as the 49ers coach. Instead of trying to establish "Physical dominance" with his running game and blockers up front, Walsh decided to do something different.

He decided he wanted his team to win the game.

More than any other coach of his generation or those that preceded him, Walsh was a devout strategist. He wanted to put his players in a position to succeed against your players and that did not necessarily mean taking on your opposite number at the point of attack and beating him one-on-one.

That certainly was one way of doing it and Walsh was not averse to using physical strength to dominate from time to time. But during the 1981 season when a 247-pound guard named Dan Audick was lining up at left tackle, Walsh never even considered strategies that called for Audick to hold his block and dominate his opposite number. That kind of thought process would be about as productive as a grown man sitting on his couch on the night of December 24 with the hope that Santa Claus would pop down the chimney with a bag full of presents.

Walsh was a thinker who used strategy to his advantage and put the fear of God in opposing coaches—a fact that none of them would admit to and must have caused many sleepless nights. Instead of trying to overpower opponents, Walsh found the favorable matchup. He threw the ball regularly on first down. He sent his receivers on short passing routes when opponents were expecting them to go long. He taught his receivers the best way to get yards after the catch, seemingly a matter of happenstance before Walsh got involved.

Walsh was at his best from a strategic sense during the 1981 championship season. The 49ers had major offensive weaknesses on the offensive line and in the backfield. Audick was undersized and often up against it when asked to block opposing defensive ends. Ricky Patton was the team's most productive running back, but all that amounted to was 543 yards and he did not even survive the team's roster cuts the following season.

It was the weakness at the running back spot that served as a catalyst for Walsh's short pass philosophy. Instead of handing the ball to his running back, he swung the ball out to them or his tight ends as extended handoffs, and that gave them the same kind of advantage a productive running game is supposed to offer.

A big part of the Niners' success that season was the ability to stack first downs. Because second-and-short and third-and-short situations predominated, the 49ers were able to do just that even if Audick was at a physical disadvantage every time he took the field.

How did Walsh overcome this issue that would have sent most coaches scouring the waiver wire or begging for a trade? He had Montana roll out to his right on a regular basis. The strategy not only allowed Audick to survive it demonstrated how accurate a passer Montana was on the move.

But the long hours Walsh put in designing game plans to take

Joe Montana and Bill Walsh smile for photographers during the closing moments of their playoff game win against the Minnesota Vikings on January 4, 1989, at Candlestick Park.

advantage of opposing teams strengths and weaknesses is what truly set him apart from his opposite numbers. During the 1981 season, Walsh and the 49ers got the best of Tom Landry and the Cowboys twice. While San Francisco was a much-improved team over the 1980 version, nobody in the NFL thought they had comparable talent to the Cowboys. Yet one of the 49ers wins was a rout and the other sent them to the Super Bowl after Dwight Clark came down with his famous catch in the corner of the end zone.

Landry was perplexed by Walsh. The man in the hat was thought to be one of the game's top innovators, but he had no clue how to deal with Walsh. He may have always had the same demeanor on the sidelines, but he was left talking to himself in the locker room after those two 1981 encounters with Walsh.

The "Finesse" label worked to the 49ers' advantage from the start. While Walsh, his coaches and players were constantly looking for strategic advantages over their opponents, they did not do so at the expense of physical play. Walsh hung a large sign in the Niners locker room that read "I WILL NOT BE OUTHIT AT ANY TIME THIS SEASON."

The physical side of the game was best represented by safety Ronnie Lott and defensive end Frod Dean, but it didn't stop there. Clark and fellow receiver Freddie Solomon got as much enjoyment from their blocking as they did catching the ball. On Clark's big plays downfield, it was almost always a Solomon block that sprung him for extra yardage. The same held true for Clark on Solomon's downfield receptions.

Eventually Walsh embellished the finesse label because he knew opponents were buying into it. Strange as it seemed as the 1981 season progressed, the 49ers used physical play to get the job done. When opponents were expecting deception, they got punched in the mouth. Then Walsh and Montana brought the hammer down with the big pass.

It was a strategy that would bring the Niners four championships throughout the 1980s and change the face of pro football.

Giving the Master His Due

Bill Walsh learned the business of coaching the pro game from Al Davis, who had learned offensive theory from Chargers coach Sid Gillman. He also spent time in Cincinnati with Paul Brown, and while they had a tempestuous personal relationship, he was clearly an influence for Walsh.

Few coaches could come close to Walsh's knowledge of the offensive game and in the case of Bears coach Mike Ditka, he underscored that disadvantage by sarcastically referring to Walsh as "The Genius."

Ditka had been a bull of a tight end in his playing career with the

Bears, Eagles, and Cowboys and had earned his coaching stripes on Tom Landry's staff in Dallas. He was about tradition, domination, defense, and the running game. If Walsh was about scripting plays and innovating, Ditka was so Old School that he was used as the cover boy on the brochure.

Ditka resented Walsh and his success. He was an especially sore loser when his team lost to the 49ers. The Ditka-Walsh standings were an even matchup, 3–3 of all time, but Ditka was at his worst following the defeats. Two of the losses were in the NFC Championship Games and the other was a 41–0 humiliation in a 1987 Monday night game that took the sheen off the Chicago franchise.

While Ditka would derisively refer to Walsh as a genius, he knew that he was going up against an offensive master. After coaching briefly in New Orleans, Iron Mike became a network television fixture on CBS and later ESPN. As he had a chance to reflect on his career, he admitted his own faults and gave credit to his peers and teachers.

Tops on Ditka's list were George Halas and Tom Landry, the two men that had told Ditka they believed in him as both a player and a coach. His admiration for both men never waned. He also had significant respect for Vince Lombardi, the architect and coach of the great Packers teams in the 1960s, often viewed as the best coach ever in any professional sport.

Ditka also opened up his perspective on Walsh. They would speak on a fairly regular basis and Ditka was deeply saddened when Walsh died in 2007. "He was a great person, a great family man, and a spectacular coach," Ditka said. "His ability to use the short passing game and put together a brilliant offense was amazing. He knew more than you did and then he knew how to take advantage of those teams. He had the benefit of great players like Joe Montana and Jerry Rice, but they had the privilege of playing under him.

"Bill Walsh was the greatest thing that ever happened to the San Francisco 49er franchise."

Ditka's turnaround on Walsh also reflected that many in the game often felt about him. He may have been a bit aloof at times but he was warm, caring and one of the most innovative football coaches ever.

Chapter 7
The Greatest Receiver of All Time

"When I saw Rice, I thought immediately of how well he would fit into our offense, and how he would give us an extra dimension."

—Bill Walsh

Discovering Rice

The Niners had their best season in 1984, finishing 15–1 and rolling to an easy Super Bowl win over the Dolphins.

Bill Walsh knew the Niners had a great team, but he also knew they could get better. He was particularly concerned about the wide receiver spot. Dwight Clark and Freddie Solomon were still talented receivers who were productive clutch performers. But Solomon was getting near the end of his career and neither wideout was a burner.

Walsh wasn't so concerned about the 1984 season but he was concerned about the future. Prior to a 49ers road game against the Houston Oilers in mid-October, Walsh was in his hotel room the night before the game watching the sports report on local television and he saw a feature on a Mississippi Valley State receiver named Jerry Rice. On that day, Rice scored five touchdowns all on plays of 50 yards or more and he finished his career with a boatload of NCAA career receiving records.

"When I saw Rice, I thought immediately of how well he would fit into our offense," Walsh said later. "And how he would give us an extra dimension."

Walsh wanted Rice badly from that moment on, but he never thought he would get a chance to select him. Even if the Niners could move up in the draft to the middle of the first round, he thought Rice would go somewhere in the first five picks.

Walsh was convinced Rice would be a star, but he had to win over a number of scouts and convince them Rice was as good as the coach believed.

One top scout even thought Rice should be no more than a sixth-round pick. There were two questions about Rice: 1) he had played at a low level, Mississippi Valley State, and nobody could be certain he would continue to excel at a much higher level; and 2) he had not run fast times in workouts, usually being timed at 4.6 for the 40, while some receivers were being tested as fast as 4.3.

Walsh relied on his own judgment. He dismissed the stop-watch, preferring what he called "football speed." His many

Jerry Rice makes a fingertip catch during Super Bowl XXIII action against the Cincinnati Bengals. The 49ers won 20–16 and Rice was named MVP after catching 11 passes for a record 215 yards.

years in the game had taught him that some players ran faster when they were making plays on the football field than when they were being timed in a sprint, and he figured Rice was one of those players. Walsh had no concerns about the level of competition either.

Walsh studied as much tape as he could get of Rice and he also relied on intelligence and psychological tests to confirm his initial evaluation. Those tests demonstrated that Rice was about as driven a college player as Walsh would ever come across.

As Walsh grew more convinced of Rice's value, other NFL teams had their doubts. Nobody wanted to swing for the fence and then whiff on a first-round pick and that's just what many feared they would do if they selected the potential star from tiny Mississippi Valley State.

The first receiver drafted was Al Toon of Wisconsin, who went to the New York Jets with the 10th pick. Eddie Brown of Miami was next to go, to Cincinnati as the 13th pick.

That got Walsh excited. He had offered his first- and second-round draft picks to any team that had been interested in trading their first-round pick. Since the Niners had won the Super Bowl, those picks were the last in each round. The only team that had shown any interest in finishing the deal was the New England Patriots and once Brown had been selected by the Bengals, Walsh made the deal with the Pats. Walsh assistant John McVay finalized the deal with Patriots general manager Dick Steinberg in the middle of the first round.

That gave the Niners the 16th pick, and they used it on Rice.

Rice had to adjust to life with the 49ers. He was somewhat overwhelmed by the huge playbook, and his mental discomfort translated to on-field problems. He dropped so many passes that newspapers were running stat boxes and television announcers were showing graphics illustrating the drop total.

But he got comfortable by the middle of his first season and he dominated the Rams by catching 10 passes for 241 yards late in the year. Those were records for 49ers rookie wideouts and it demonstrated what life would be like in years to come.

Jerry Rice and Super Bowl XXIII

The Super Bowl is where players make their reputations.

It may not be fair to everyone, because there are loads of examples of great players who never make it to the big game— Barry Sanders, John Brodie, Eric Dickerson, Dick Butkus, and Deacon Jones, to name a few. But to a large majority of football fans, if a star player hasn't done it in the Super Bowl he hasn't done it at all.

Jerry Rice is widely recognized as the greatest wide receiver to play the game. Many of his supporters make the argument that Rice is the greatest player at any position. Rice was at his best in each of his three Super Bowl appearances with the Niners.

San Francisco already had two Super Bowl titles when Rice was drafted out of Mississippi Valley State in 1985 and they remained a very solid team in his first three years, although they were not as dominant as they had been and were unable to win the NFC playoffs.

However, the 1988 season was quite special for the Niners, winning the NFC West with a 10–6 record and beating the Vikings and the Bears in the NFC playoffs to win a spot in Super Bowl XXIII in Miami against the Bengals.

The win over Chicago was especially notable. Not only did the Niners go on the road to defeat the Bears, they did it in severe weather conditions. At the time, the Bears were thought to be an indomitable team in the elements, having thrived under head coach Mike Ditka in freezing conditions that Chicago fans referred to as "Bear weather."

Of all the opponents the Bears fans wanted to come to Chicago when the windchill registered minus-26, the Niners were at the top of the list.

Right or wrong, the Niners were perceived as a finesse team that would fall apart in harsh winter conditions. They were described by glib talk-show hosts, like windbag Chet Coppock, as "wine drinkers" and "quiche eaters."

While the Bears put on a pregame show that saw veteran

tough guys Steve McMichael and Dan Hampton go through warmups in shirtsleeves while the Niners dressed in more layers than Nanook of the North, the Niners were the ones who played like men once the game started.

Rice was particularly impressive, scoring twice on 61-yard and 27-yard TD receptions. Rice may not have had a lot of experience playing in brutal weather, but he quickly discovered he had a major advantage over the defensive backs who tried to stay with him.

"The field was not in good shape at all," Rice recalled. "There were some parts of it that were torn up and some that were frozen. I knew where I was going and they didn't. Every time I made a cut I was able to open some distance. It worked out pretty well."

Pretty well turned out to be a 28–3 win in the NFC title game. It also marked the end of the Bears as a championship contender in the NFL.

The Niners were thought to have an advantage against the Bengals, but head coach Bill Walsh told everyone who would listen that Sam Wyche had a very strong team and it would take the Niners' best game to beat them. Walsh was concerned with Cincinnati's advantage on special teams and their pounding ground attack.

He was confident that Montana, Rice, and John Taylor could move the ball, but the Niners had a battle on their hands on both sides of the line of scrimmage. Walsh thought the game could come down to the fourth quarter and said so before the game during myriad media press conferences. Few of the reporters on hand believed him. Most thought the Niners from the much stronger NFC would win easily.

Rice knew his coach was not just blowing smoke. As a matter of fact, he had doubts about his own ability to play his best game because he re-aggravated an ankle injury during practice and was unable to go at full speed.

"There was no way I would have ever missed the game," Rice said. "I hurt my ankle on the Monday before the game and it was very uncomfortable. But I have an excellent work ethic and I would never miss a game I could play—let alone the Super Bowl!"

The game did not go well for the Niners in the early going. Huge tackle Steve Wallace broke his ankle on the third play of the game and the offense was unable to find its rhythm.

The score was a shocking 3–3 at halftime and when Stanford Jennings brought back a kickoff 93 yards in the third quarter, San Francisco was on the short end of a 13–6 score. That play seemed to kick-start the Niners, who knew they had no more time to waste.

San Francisco took over possession on its own 15 and Montana worked the ball to Rice, and Roger Craig out of the backfield for 40 more as they drove for 31 yards up the field. The drive culminated when Montana hit Rice with a 14-yard touchdown pass early in the fourth quarter, tying the game at 13–13.

Cincinnati would not go away. The Bengals were able to put together a clutch drive of their own and Jim Breech gave them the lead once again when he kicked a 40-yard field goal. All the Bengals had to do was keep the Niners from scoring over the final 3:20 and they would be world champions.

Of course, that would not be an easy task; ultimately it would prove impossible. Cincinnati head coach Sam Wyche had his team put all its attention on Rice on the final drive, but the strategy still proved fruitless. The Bengals forced the Niners to start the drive from their own 8-yard line, but it proved to be just a minor factor that would add to the drama.

There was tension in the Niners huddle as they took the field for the final drive, but none of it was coming from Montana. As if to prove he was oblivious to the moment, he pointed to the stands and said, "Isn't that John Candy?"

It was indeed the hefty comedic actor and the moment served its purpose. Those who had been a bit tense were ready to do their job once again. Montana was razor sharp on the drive, throwing passes to Roger Craig, John Frank, and Jerry Rice to move the ball quickly downfield. However, a penalty on center Randy Cross for being illegally downfield backed the Niners up to the Cincinnati 45.

It was second-and-20 and the Niners needed a big play if they were going to get in position to try a tying field goal. Rice ran a square-in route over the middle, and even though the Bengals attempted to cover him with three men—Lewis Billups, David Fulcher, and Ray Horton—the brilliant Rice came open. Montana's pass hit him in stride and ran the ball another 14 yards after catching it for a 27-yard gain.

The Niners were no longer thinking about tying the game. They wanted the win in regulation. An eight-yard pass from Montana to Craig gave San Francisco a second-and-two at the Bengals' 10.

It was all over at that moment. The entire stadium knew that the combination of Montana and Rice would close out the game. Walsh had the Bengals right where he wanted them. He knew Wyche would sell his soul if he could stop Rice on the play, so he called "20 Halfback Curl X Up" for Roger Craig. Rice went into motion and took coverage with him. Craig was unable to get free from the jam, but John Taylor had found a seam and Montana quickly let it go in his direction. The pass hit Taylor in stride and the Niners had their third Super Bowl victory—and their second over the Bengals.

"It was just a great moment," said Rice. "I didn't make that catch but it felt just like I did. To see your teammate succeed and to know that you played a huge role in making that happen was just a wonderful feeling. I couldn't have been any happier if I had made the catch."

Rice clearly had a career filled with mind-boggling performances. But this may very well have been his best: catching 11 balls for 215 yards and one touchdown and being named the Super Bowl MVP.

It also shed light on Taylor, who may have been the most underrated player on the great Niners team. Taylor caught 347 passes for 5,598 yards and 43 touchdowns over his nine-year career and made as many clutch receptions for the Niners as anyone not named Rice. Taylor also blocked like a demon, a fact that helped Rice and Craig break many long plays.

But even without Taylor, Rice would still be recognized as the greatest receiver the game has known. He was never better than in the 1988 postseason, a fact that the Vikings, Bears, and Bengals know all too well.

Chapter 8
New Coach, Similar Results

The real credit to George is that he didn't come in and try to put his personal stamp on everything, that he wasn't so insecure that everything had to be his way or no way."

—Eric Wright

George Seifert Takes Charge

The 49ers' achievements have been glorified over the years. Five Super Bowl championships will do that to a team. Bill Walsh is a football demigod. Joe Montana and Steve Young are two of the most prominent members in the Hall of Fame. Jerry Rice is widely considered the best receiver in NFL history and perhaps the best player to ever don a jersey. Hard-hitting Ronnie Lott is another legend. Lott is a man who was so tough he was willing to lose a piece of his pinky finger in order to keep on playing.

In the front office, names like Eddie DeBartolo, Carmen Policy, and John McVay have a special place in the city's heart for making the moves that have kept the team on top for so many years.

Now let's talk about George Seifert. He led the 49ers to two of their Super Bowl titles and was widely responsible for building a great defense. But for some reason history has not looked kindly upon Seifert. He has become a forgotten man whose accomplishments have been largely dismissed.

How many NFL coaches have won a Super Bowl in their first season? Bill Walsh, Bill Parcells, Joe Gibbs, and Bill Belichick can't make that claim. Seifert can, but the achievement gets pushed aside and dismissed because he inherited Walsh's Super Bowl champion team.

Five years later Seifert's team won another Super Bowl with an offense that has to be considered one of the strongest the game has ever seen. Seifert, however, gets no credit. He made his bones as a defensive game planner and a fine evaluator of talent on that side of the ball. But as far as the offense was concerned, give the credit to Young and offensive coordinator Mike Shanahan. Seifert? Seifert was just lucky to be driving the bus.

How ridiculous. Certainly he was able to take advantage of Walsh's ability to procure talent. But when it came to leadership Seifert had his own style and it was very effective.

Throughout his first season, Seifert heard the comparisons with Walsh. He heard how Walsh said that this was the best 49ers team in the organization's history. He heard how the 49ers' successful,

The Niners stayed on track when George Seifert took over for Bill Walsh in 1989. They defended their Super Bowl title and continued to be a major force for a year.

machinelike organization would slip without Walsh. He heard how he lacked the pizzazz and showmanship of an NFL coach and would succumb to the rigors of the job. He listened. He conquered.

"There's no way from time to time that I couldn't be aware of all the things being said, but I just tried to stay focused on the games," Seifert said prior to the Niners' appearance in Super Bowl XXIV. "I developed most as a coach under Bill. I have the highest regard for him as a friend."

One of the things that Seifert did for his players in 1989 was to improve the atmosphere. Walsh may have been a brilliant strategist and leader, but he often made players very uncomfortable with his demanding and threatening ways. When Seifert was made head coach, he appreciated his players and they seemed to feel the same way about him, even when they disagreed with him.

"First of all, George is a really nice man," said former 49ers cornerback Eric Wright. "He is a very good person and a very intelligent person. He is a workaholic and a loner. [You] never really knew George that well or how he was going to be as a head coach. He talked more in his first year as head coach than he had in the nine years before put together. The guys on the defense knew how he handled them individually, but we wondered how George was going to handle this team as a group.

"The real credit to George is that he didn't come in and try to put his personal stamp on everything, that he wasn't so insecure that everything had to be his way or no way."

Wright said that Seifert knew offensive football "from the unique perspective of being a defensive wizard," but allowed Montana to assert his seasoned understandings and abilities in a way that Walsh never did.

Matt Millen, who would go on to a career in broadcasting before being hired as team president of the Detroit Lions, was also impressed with Seifert's leadership abilities.

"George has Joe Paterno's perspective and a focus that ensures that if he does step in a hole, it sure won't be the one right in front of him," Millen said. "He has Tom Flores's discipline on the field of letting his players play and not toying with them. I remember being with the Raiders when we played the 49ers and won. Before the game, I was wondering what in the world Bill Walsh was trying to do to Joe Montana, having jerked him in and out of games and warming up Steve Young on the sidelines in several games.

"Now, Steve Young is a good quarterback and I may be insulting all the Walsh fans out there, but let's get serious. Joe didn't deserve that and George recognized it and seemed to tell Joe, 'Look, you go play, I'll watch.' When people say it was Bill Walsh's team, that's ridiculous. Give Bill all the credit in the world for what he achieved, but realize that when George came in it was a different team with new personalities playing under different circumstances. It was definitely Seifert's team."

Cornerback Tim McKyer was very critical of Seifert from time to time, but he still had respect for his leadership. "We've had our differences, but I will give him credit for this: by keeping things a lot the same and not being tyrannical, he has let the players make the system and made the 49ers continue to be winners."

Seifert had a different approach than most head coaches. His ego did not have to be appeased and he needed no strokes. When it came to credit, he handed it out to his players and assistants—and would not take any himself.

"George's approach was like that of an assistant coach," said Bobb McKittrick, the 49ers' offensive line coach who died in 2000. "He is blue-collar and down to earth, honest and frank. He's not flashy; he'd rather fish while you hear about a lot of coaches golfing in Hawaii or playing tennis in Cancun. I've been around a lot of head coaches, but George is the first one who was ever this way: every Monday morning after a big win, George's first words to the team were, 'Men, congratulations on your win.' Not *my* win or even *our* win but *your* win. It's an easy thing to say, but I'd never heard it said. It kind of sums up his way."

The 49ers added defensive backs Dave Waymer from the Saints and Hanford Dixon of the Browns late in their careers. Both came to the 49ers during the summer of 1990 and were impressed with Seifert's interpersonal skills and on-field demeanor.

"You're talking about a guy who is intense," said Waymer, who spent two years with the Niners before finishing his career in Oakland in 1992. "He is also smart and combines those two characteristics in an unusual way. He knows where everybody on the field belongs."

"He understands a lot about the game and even more about players," said Dixon before being released by the team. "This is a relaxed but a very serious, working atmosphere. That's very important and very hard to come by."

The results in the 1989 season were remarkable from start to finish. The Niners were 14–2 in the regular season and then swept through the playoffs. Their season was culminated by a 55–10 win over the Broncos in Super Bowl XXIV.

The offense no longer depended on just the Montana-to-Jerry Rice combination. The offense spread the ball around and scored points by the bucket load.

The defense became sharper and more efficient. The Niners gave up just 26 points in the postseason. And when disciplinary action was needed, Seifert reacted swiftly and convincingly, challenging some players and suspending others.

More than anything, he skillfully handled each comparison to Walsh, complimenting Walsh each step of the way and never succumbing to the pressures of filling Walsh's shoes.

Rice felt a tremendous loyalty to Walsh for finding him, drafting him, and playing him. However, he came to appreciate the graceful way Seifert moved to the head coaching position.

"Anyone would be lying if they didn't say there was pressure on George from every circle," Rice said. "Bill left this organization with a winning attitude. The players couldn't believe Bill retired. It was like, 'Man, the legend is over.' When you thought of the San Francisco 49ers, you thought of Bill Walsh. There was something special about Bill; maybe it was the white, silver hair. He could get the best out of you, though.

"When George took over, it was clear that he had that same ability. The players had mixed feelings about Bill because he did not communicate with everyone. He would pick his players and let them get the message to the rest of the team. George communicates with everyone, and everyone appreciates that."

Unlike many NFL coaches, Seifert was not interested in maximizing his power base and dominating the media. He was much happier in his off-the-field moments than most of his peers. He had other interests and was not consumed by the coaching profession.

Seifert was a longtime fisherman and he had stories. While fishing with friends for striped bass in the Pacific Ocean in the mid-1980s, his boat capsized. Seifert and his group swam nearly 300 yards safely to shore. A week later, he was back fishing near the same spot.

"You get close to the waves and throw your rod in there and there's plenty of fish," he said. "It's exciting, like falling off the trampoline and getting back on it again. The real fear wasn't the water but the boat coming down on top of you. I always liked to go out there in the weeks before camp started just to get my mind prepared for what was about to come."

Getting the Job

In January 1989, Seifert was on his way to Cleveland to interview for the Browns' head coaching job. His flight, which had a scheduled stop in Dallas, was going to be delayed in Dallas because of bad weather in Cleveland, so Seifert used an in-plane telephone to alert his wife, who was at home in the Bay Area. She told him that when he arrived in Dallas he should turn around and come home. The 49ers wanted him as head coach. Of course, Seifert kept the secret. "On the plane to Dallas, I was going over my game plan, what I would say in the interview and what I would ask. And then on the flight back home, I was excited and anxious. But I didn't talk to anyone. I just had a glass of white wine."

Walsh had been campaigning for Seifert to get the head coaching job as soon as the Niners had defeated the Bengals in Super Bowl XXIII. He had to convince DeBartolo that Seifert was the right man for the job. Seifert had been nearly as innovative on the defensive side of the ball as Walsh had been on offense, and the two had formed a great partnerships. Since Mike Holmgren was the offensive coordinator and he was one of the sharpest minds in the business, Seifert would be the ideal leader.

But DeBartolo wanted to make a bigger splash. With Walsh out, he wanted to turn his attention to Jimmy Johnson, who was widely perceived as the best coach in college football. He had led the Miami Hurricanes to the national championship and helped make them an every-season contender and he had a certain charisma that Seifert lacked.

But Walsh looked at Johnson as a bit of a country bumpkin who would not be able to handle the complexity of the 49ers offense. Walsh told DeBartolo if he was insistent on going outside the organization he needed to take a long, hard look at UCLA head coach Terry Donahue, who was a bit more sophisticated than Johnson.

Finally, DeBartolo relented and hired Seifert.

The move also motivated the 49ers players who wanted to show they could win without Walsh. They had nothing against their old coach but he had gotten more than his fair share of the credit and he was, after all, "the Genius." With Walsh off to the broadcast booth, the 49ers now had an opportunity to get full credit for the success of the team.

The Walsh Backlash

Nobody on the team wanted to succeed more without Walsh than Ronnie Lott. Lott carried a seething resentment of Walsh dating back to the strike season of 1987. It had to do with loyalty, and Lott felt that Walsh hadn't demonstrated his because he publicly supported the "Minor Niners" who came into replace the players on the picket line. Walsh did it to help pressure the players into ending the strike and to help his new players feel as if they belonged as a part of the organization, but his attitude left a bitter taste when the players returned.

Lott was also angry that Walsh hadn't shared his retirement

plans with his players. They found out about it the same way the fans did—through a press conference a few days after the Super Bowl win over the Bengals.

Publicly, Lott hid his emotions. He told reporters that winning without Walsh created a "new challenge" for the team. Privately, he was more emotional than ever and taking an even greater role in stoking the inner fire of his teammates than he had before. Lott had always been an emotional leader, but it was clear that the intensity was even higher than it had ever been.

Seifert had always thought Lott was a remarkable individual. Not only was he thoroughly prepared every time he took the field, he had an attitude that he had to leave his imprint on every hit he made. Bringing a ball carrier down was not enough. If he had a clean shot at a running back or receiver, he had to hit with everything he had or he felt he was not giving his all to his teammates or himself.

The results were dramatic and nobody appreciated that more than Seifert. "I've seen big hits rev up a team before," said Seifert. "But I've never seen it have the impact as when Ronnie brings it. We'll be at a certain level and playing well, but when Lott hits someone it changes the whole chemistry out there. The level of play gets raised to a different level and we start to dominate. This was not just a once-in-a-while type of thing either. Just about every time he made one of those hits, it translated to the rest of the team. As a coach, you can't ask for any more than that."

The 49ers were coming off their third Super Bowl title when Walsh left and Seifert stepped in. The team had failed the year after their first two titles and everybody in the locker room knew it. The Niners were determined to show that they could repeat their success or at least play much better than they had in 1982 or 1985 (11th place in strike season and wild-card losers, respectively).

There was no chance of that happening to the 49ers in 1989. Fueled by Lott's passion and Montana's excellence, the Niners cruised to a 14–2 regular season record. It seemed as though they could do whatever they wanted on the field at any time, and that careful analysis of two games showed that the rest of the league could not compete.

San Francisco head coach George Seifert and ex-49ers head coach Bill Walsh share a chat after the team's Super Bowl workout in Santa Clara on January 20, 1990. This was Walsh's first visit to the 49ers camp in several weeks, and he joked with the media that he was taking over.

In Week 3, the 49ers traveled to Philadelphia to take on Buddy Ryan's Eagles. Ryan, of course, was a fiery leader who liked nothing better than destroying sophisticated offensive play. He was an old-school ex–drill sergeant who believed that real men played defense and offense was just a necessary evil. He had been the architect of the Chicago Bears' "46" defense during their championship season in 1985 and he was just as famous for his feud with Chicago head coach Mike Ditka as he was his own team's excellence.

He also had no use for the 49ers. He was no fan of Walsh's professorial ways and didn't have much use for Seifert either. When Ryan's Eagles rolled to 21–10 early in the fourth quarter, the rotund Ryan was truly enjoying his afternoon.

The Eagles had used a fierce pass rush to stifle the 49ers attack. Led by Reggie White and Jerome Brown, the Eagles sacked Montana eight times through the first three quarters. But instead of going into protection mode and realizing they had 13 regular-season games left, the Niners put on an amazing show and Montana threw four fourth-quarter TD passes to give the Niners a 38–28 victory.

San Francisco lost its next game to the Los Angeles Rams, 13–12, and would only lose one more until they played the Rams again in a Week 15 Monday night game in Los Angeles. In that game, the greatness of Montana and number two receiver John Taylor would shock the football world. Taylor caught two 90-plus-yard TD passes (92 and 96 yards) as the Niners took a come-from-behind 30–27 decision.

Taylor's ability showed that it was not just the Montana-Rice show. Taylor and tight end Brent Jones were both big-play threats. Stopping Rice—which was nearly impossible to begin with—was no longer the answer to slowing down the Niners. They had multiple threats, and that allowed Montana to complete 70.2 percent of his passes and set an NFL record with a passer rating of 112.4.

The playoffs proved to be a walk-over. San Francisco annihilated Minnesota 41–13, setting up the only postseason meeting between the 49ers and Rams in the two teams' history. Since they had split a pair of close regular-season games—with the Rams winning in San Francisco—many expected this game to be close. But after giving up an early field goal, it was all San Francisco. The 30–3 Niner victory featured another brilliant performance by Montana, as he completed 26 of 30 passes.

That win put the Niners in Super Bowl XXIV against the Broncos. The oddsmakers had made the Niners heavy favorites and the facts backed up that choice. The NFC was in the midst of 13 straight Super Bowl victories and was clearly the dominant conference. Few thought the Broncos could compete, but the enormity of the rout was both awe-inspiring and humiliating.

Chapter 9
Pounding the Broncos for Another Championship

"I think John [Elway] really has that burden hanging over his head, whether it's deserved or not.... And what an opponent, what a situation for him to be in to win."

—Charlie Waters, before Denver's loss to the 49ers in Super Bowl XXIV

John Elway's Burden

The John Elway story ultimately finished as one of the great ones in NFL history. After three painful defeats in the Super Bowl, he closed out his brilliant career with back-to-back championships. The Broncos ended the NFC's 13-year domination of the event by beating the Packers 31–24 in Super Bowl XXXII in San Diego and then defending their title with a 34–19 win over an outmanned Atlanta Falcons team in Miami.

But prior to those two games, Elway's season always ended in frustration, with either a defeat in the playoffs or Super Bowl or not even making the playoffs.

The most memorable of those defeats was the abject humiliation the team suffered in Super Bowl XXIV in New Orleans at the hands of the 49ers.

San Francisco rolled into the Super Bowl with a 14–2 regular-season record and one-sided wins over the Vikings and Rams in the playoffs. The team appeared unstoppable, motivated to defend the Super Bowl title they had earned the year before against the Bengals. They also wanted to show the world they could win a title without Bill Walsh, who had been given the title of "the Genius" for the cerebral and outstanding way he ran the team during his 10 years.

Walsh had no doubt earned the credit and praise that had come his way, but 49ers players like Ronnie Lott, Roger Craig, Tom Rathman, and Keena Turner had a desire to win one without him.

That combination of talent and motivation would lead to a blowout of epic proportions in the Super Bowl. The Broncos had a nice team with Elway at quarterback, Dan Reeves at head coach, and decent role players, but they lacked the size, strength, speed, and athleticism to compete with the Niners. And they appeared to know it before the game started.

While the 49ers expressed confidence in their ability to win the game in all phases during the media sessions prior to the game, the Bronco players used phrases like "you never know what can happen" and "if we get a few early breaks this could go our way."

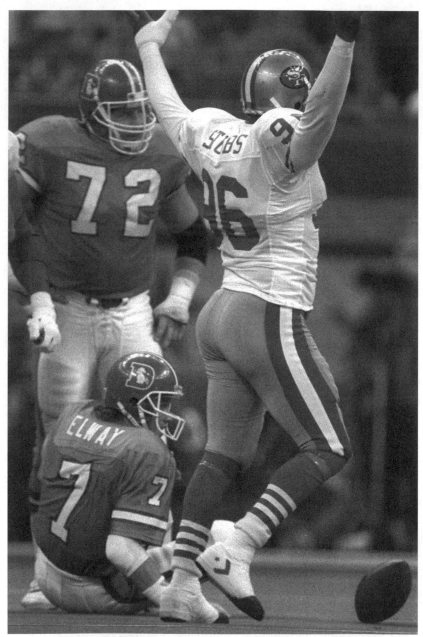

Daniel Stubbs celebrates after sacking Denver Broncos quarterback John Elway during fourth quarter action at Super Bowl XXIV in New Orleans on January 28, 1990. The 49ers stomped Denver 55–10.

Nobody appeared to know it more than Elway, who was also facing a bitter off-season if the Broncos lost. He would become a three-time loser in the Super Bowl, a fate he would share at the time only with former Viking quarterback Fran Tarkenton. Buffalo's Jim Kelly would later lose four consecutive Super Bowls.

Though Elway would ultimately erase that label at the end of his career, it would be an albatross for him for many years. Such simplistic labels are a basic part of sports and they almost always provide an incomplete story. The Broncos were almost always a one-dimensional team in those years, wholly dependent on Elway and a small but overachieving group of defenders. They had been taken apart in previous Super Bowls by the Giants and the Redskins. Both of those teams had big, strong defenses, dominating ground games, and opportunistic passing games. Both games were similar in that Denver jumped out to early leads but was overwhelmed relatively quickly.

Elway said all the right things before the game and tried to give the impression that the Broncos had a chance to compete on even terms with the Niners.

"I feel fortunate this is the third time I've had a chance in four years," he said. "You just never know how many chances you're going to get in your career. I felt that we let two go by, and I'd hate to see a third go by. It seems that monkey is getting bigger."

His teammates and coaches knew Elway faced pressure because of the two earlier Super Bowl defeats. "I think John really has that burden hanging over his head, whether it's deserved or not," said Charlie Waters, the Denver defensive secondary coach and a former teammate of Roger Staubach with the Dallas Cowboys. "John knows this is his chance for the Hall of Fame. And what an opponent, what a situation for him to be in to win. But he really believes he can do it. He believes he's on right now."

Elway said the greatness of the opponent removed all pressure from the equation. At least those were the words that came out of his mouth. "There's no pressure on us," Elway said. "There is, but there isn't. When no one gives you a chance, you can go out and let it fly."

Super Bowl XXIV would make the defeats to the Giants and Redskins look like picnics for the Denver organization.

The 49ers were 11-point favorites and they made sure there would be no upset. Almost immediately, Montana hit Rice with a 20-yard TD pass. The Broncos came back with a 42-yard field goal from bare-footed kicker David Treadwell, but that would be the last bit of fight shown by the team. Montana found Brent Jones with a seven-yard pass and the Niners had a 13–3 lead at the end of a quarter.

The Niners defense started turning up the heat on Elway and he would be under pressure for the rest of the game. He was sacked six times and intercepted twice. Tom Rathman added a one-yard TD in the second quarter and when Rice scored on a 38-yard pass from Montana shortly before halftime for a 27–3 lead, the only question that remained was how large the margin would eventually get.

In the regular season, when teams build three-touchdown leads by halftime the rest of the game is normally about holding on to the ball and keeping the opponent at bay. But in the Super Bowl, there is no such etiquette. The Niners continued to attack in the third quarter and Montana threw TD passes to Rice and John Taylor. The Broncos would finally get into the end zone on a three-yard run by Elway but that only led to two fourth-quarter rushing touchdowns by Rathman and Roger Craig. Final score: 49ers 55, Broncos 10.

While it was the largest margin of victory in Super Bowl history, the Niners could have laid it on even more had they chosen to do so.

Instead of an NFL championship game, it had all the appearances of a one-sided boxing match that ended in an early knockout. Elway knew from the start that his team had been overwhelmed and really had no chance. But that didn't stop the rest of the football world from questioning him on how good he really was. He had lost three Super Bowls in three opportunities and done so in ignominious fashion.

The painful defeats weighed on him for another eight years until the Broncos defeated Green Bay 31–24 in Super Bowl XXXII in

San Diego. That was the game that would remove the doubt that had stained Elway's legacy—and much of that doubt had been established by a marauding and talented group of 49ers.

Trash-Talking Gone Wrong

You didn't have to be a football expert to know that the Niners had a huge advantage when they took the field in Super Bowl XXIV against the Broncos.

They were bigger, stronger, more athletic, and more talented. They came from the far more talented NFC and they had Joe Montana and Jerry Rice.

Even the most ardent Bronco supporters knew their team would be lucky to stay in the game against such a juggernaut, and it appeared some Bronco players and coaches seemed to know it as well.

But that did not apply to Denver's hard-hitting pair of safeties. Dennis Smith and Steve Atwater had given the Bronco defense an identity. Receivers and running backs who ventured into the Denver secondary were going to cross paths with two of the nastiest safeties in the game. Neither one was interested in simply making the tackle. They wanted to leave an imprint—physical and emotional—on those who trespassed into their territory.

That's a great attitude and Smith and Atwater fed off each other. If Smith made a big play, Atwater would do the loudest howling. If Atwater made a big hit, Smith would get stoked and couldn't wait for his next big hit.

In most circumstances, that's an attribute for a pair of football players. But when those players are getting set to line up in the Super Bowl against the 49ers and their primary responsibility is containing Rice, those veterans need to learn how to rein in their excess verbiage.

But Smith and Atwater were not about to rein anything in. Even before the game they were hammering at Rice verbally. They claimed that neither Rice nor John Taylor were tough enough to catch the ball in the Denver secondary and then hold on to it after

Jerry Rice shakes off Denver Broncos defender Dennis Smith during the 49ers' 55–10 victory in Super Bowl XXIV.

absorbing a big hit. Nobody believed either man, but they continued to woof throughout Super Bowl week and into pregame warmups.

Rice was the last player in the world to back down. He trained six to eight hours a day in the off-season so he would be in the best possible shape whenever a big moment arrived. Question his toughness? That was fine with Rice. It just gave him more fuel as he prepared for the Broncos.

"Their comments got me all fired up," Rice said. "They acted as if me and John were some kind of rookies and didn't know what to expect."

Rice set the tone for the game on the opening drive. San Francisco had no problems moving the ball and found themselves at the Denver 20. Montana had Rice run over the middle and the 220-pound Atwater was right on his heels as Rice brought the ball in. Atwater lunged after Rice, hoping to leave him plastered all over the field and separated from the football.

Rice felt the hit and it was fairly substantial contact. But Atwater was so concerned with keeping up with Rice and delivering the big hit that he did not wrap up his attempted tackle. Rice bounced out of Atwater's grasp and easily made it into the end zone.

"He tried to unload on me," Rice said. "But usually when you are trying to deliver the big hit you don't wrap up. He hit fairly hard but I was not about to go down."

Rice did not turn around, wag the ball in Atwater's face, and start to woof. Instead, he celebrated with his teammates and flipped the ball to the official.

"When you score a touchdown on the first drive, that means a lot more than trash talking," Rice said. "I knew they were hurting plenty and giving up the touchdown was painful enough for them."

It only got worse from there as Atwater and Smith were forced to eat their own words…along with the 45-point defeat.

Chapter 10
Transition at Quarterback

"I never thought it was my team. I didn't feel that it was my role to go around the locker room and tell everybody what to do. But once I started to play regularly, I could do that."

—Steve Young

Steve Young Gets His Opportunity

Steve Young ranks up there with the great quarterbacks of the game. Open up the NFL record book and his name is prominently listed.

He led the league in passing six times in his career, matching Sammy Baugh for the most times accomplishing that feat in NFL history. Young led the league four straight times, and no other quarterback has done it more than three consecutive times. He is the all-time career leader in passer rating, ahead of Peyton Manning, Kurt Warner, and yes, Joe Montana.

His achievements and records are numerous but for everything he accomplished, Young was often treated like an unwelcome guest in his own home.

Young was not an ogre, nor did he have a Barry Bonds–like personality. He was cordial and helpful to the media and just as warm to his teammates, coaches, and fans. But he did have one fault: he was not Montana.

Talk to many experts around the game and Montana's name comes up as much as anyone's. When it comes to the game's greatest quarterback, Montana is always in the forefront of the discussion.

Many would mention John Elway, Dan Marino, Brett Favre, or Johnny Unitas, but Montana got as many votes as any of them. He led the Niners to four Super Bowl titles and he earned undying loyalty for bringing that glory to the city and the franchise.

Going into the 1994 season, Young had played as well as any quarterback in the game but he had not won a Super Bowl title. He knew that winning the title would decide his legacy—both in the minds of the fans and in his own.

"Whether you like it or not, one of the primary ways you are measured is through your titles," said Young. "Especially for a quarterback—and especially when you play for this team."

There was more than a bit of tension between Montana and Young when they were both teammates on the Niners. It was understandable, considering both had tremendous competitive instincts and both wanted to play. But it seemed that Montana

Steve Young (8) eludes Charles Mann of the Washington Redskins to scramble for a first-half first down during the NFC conference semifinal game on a rain-soaked Candlestick Park field in January 1993.

used his status as one of the game's elite players to snub Young on more than an occasional basis. Young never allowed these insults to escalate into a full-blown war between the two, and that is a remarkable testimony to the class he had throughout his career.

But it was the 1994 season in which Young overcame his demons, as thoroughly in charge of the team as Montana had been in his second season with the Kansas City Chiefs.

The Niners offense was particularly loaded with explosive players like Jerry Rice, Ricky Watters, Brent Jones, and John Taylor available as receivers.

The 1994 Niners proved to be one of the best offensive teams in NFL history, but it was in early-season losses to the Chiefs and Eagles that the Niners came of age. In both games, Young was battered brutally by the opposing defenses but he never looked for the easy way out. The loss to the Chiefs—quarterbacked by Montana—had to be particularly galling, but it was in the 40–8 home loss to the Eagles that he showed his mettle.

It was clearly Philadelphia's day and they were treating Young with a sense of brutality as defensive end Reggie White had basically taken up residence in the 49ers backfield and punished Young every time he got his hands on him. As the game got out of hand, head coach George Seifert was left with no choice but to replace him with Elvis Grbac.

The only problem was that Seifert didn't clear it with his quarterback. Despite the physical abuse, Young had never even considered coming out of the game. He was not shy about letting Seifert know that he was displeased. He gave his coach an earful on the sidelines and that was the final bit of evidence needed to convince the Montana loyalists on the team that Young was a great leader. Not only did Young want to stay in the game, he also stood up for himself because he knew the move would be interpreted that the big loss was his fault.

"It was a very key moment," said Niners offensive lineman Jesse Sapolu. "Nobody could have blamed Steve if he had wanted to come out of the game. But to go off the way he did when the coach made the decision to take him out showed everybody how much he wanted it. He was a great quarterback who had the kind of desire and ethic that matched his talent. That's awfully tough to beat."

Sapolu wasn't joking. The Niners reeled off 10 straight wins and wouldn't lose again until they dropped a meaningless final week game at Minnesota. By that time, the Niners had won the NFC West and secured home-field advantage throughout the NFC playoffs.

The week after the loss to the Eagles, the Niners fell behind Detroit 14–0 and it seemed they were on their way to another defeat. He took a brutal hit in the first half and was barely able to crawl off the field. When it looked like he might be relegated to the bench the rest of the game, Young willed himself back on to the field and led San Francisco to a 27–21 victory.

As the 49ers punctuated the regular season with a 21–15 win over the Cowboys, they knew they would see the Cowboys again in the NFC championship. After a perfunctory 44–14 demolition of the Bears in the divisional playoffs, the Cowboys were unable to compete with the Niners. Deion Sanders gave the 49ers a much-needed boost against Cowboys receiver Michael Irvin and Young and Rice led the Niners to a big offensive day. With San Francisco taking command, Dallas quarterback Troy Aikman was forced to throw on nearly every down. It was a game plan that neither Aikman nor head coach Jimmy Johnson knew the Cowboys could live with. By the time the long game had finally ended, San Francisco walked away with a 38–28 win that really was not that close.

That game had ostensibly been the true Super Bowl. The San Diego Chargers had enjoyed a nice run to get to Miami and represent the AFC, but there was no way the Chargers had the firepower to hang in with the Niners.

The execution of the game plan was just as brutal as many of the observers had anticipated. Young threw TD passes to Rice and Watters before the game was five minutes old and the Niners just rolled.

The 49ers had a 28–10 halftime lead and built their margin to 32 points in the second half. Young was simply brilliant, completing 24 of 36 passes for 325 yards and set a Super Bowl record with six touchdown passes—three of them to Rice. But it wasn't just Young's passing that got the job done. He had 49 rushing yards and made plays with his feet whenever the overmatched Chargers thought they might be able to hem him in.

After the game, Young earned the Super Bowl MVP trophy for the victorious Niners. Elated with the win and his own performance, Young had teammate Harris Barton help him remove an imaginary monkey from his back. The title that he needed to confirm his greatness had been well earned and he was not going to let the moment pass without a ceremony.

Montana would always be a legendary Bay Area hero, but that game gave Young the same status. He no longer had to prove anything to the doubters because his own championship team had been impressive. Young had stepped out of Montana's shadow and he now had his own legion of fans to help him celebrate his great moment.

The Cowboys' Perspective

There is no doubt that Jimmy Johnson is one of the greatest coaches to step on a football field.

He made a name for himself by taking a low-profile Oklahoma State football team and building a successful program. He was quickly snatched up by the University of Miami when Howard Schnellenberger retired and helped turn the Hurricanes into a national power. Johnson won one national championship and his team played for another during his five-year run.

His star continued to soar when Jerry Jones bought the Dallas Cowboys and he hired Johnson to replace the legendary Tom Landry. While Jones and Johnson would eventually have an explosive divorce, Johnson would win two Super Bowl titles with his great Cowboys team.

Throughout the late 1980s and into the mid-1990s, the NFC was clearly the dominant conference. The Cowboys and the Niners were almost always the two best teams in the NFC and the winner of those titanic postseason clashes always emerged as Super Bowl champions.

Johnson's Cowboys defeated Young and his 49ers teammates in the 1992 and 1993 NFC Championship Games, but the Niners turned things around in the 1994 NFC title game. By that time Johnson had left the Cowboys as Jones and Johnson could no longer stomach each other.

Johnson knew that he was facing one of the greatest quarterbacks in the game when they defeated the Niners, and he knew his old team was in trouble when the 49ers had earned home-field advantage in the 1994 NFC Championship Game.

"I think the key to the Niners finally beating the Cowboys in that NFC Championship Game was their meeting in November [November 13] when the Niners won the game and got a leg up for home-field advantage," Johnson said. "If the Cowboys had won that game and the NFC title game was in Dallas, it might have been a different story.

"But even if the game had been in Dallas, the Cowboys would have had to beat a great quarterback in Steve Young. There was so much growth to his game that season. Dallas had the number one pass defense in the league that year, so it showed great maturity on Steve's part not to try and get it all done with his arm."

Young only threw for 155 yards in a game the 49ers won 38–28. He threw a big touchdown pass to Jerry Rice before halftime to give the Niners control of the game and made good decisions with the football throughout.

"Steve didn't throw an interception in the game and he was able to pick up important yardage on the ground. He eliminated negative plays without toning down his explosive ability. To me, that's how he really became an outstanding quarterback."

Johnson said he was not above playing a little gamesmanship with Young when he was coaching against him. He said he knew he had to look for every advantage when facing a quarterback as great as Young.

"People tried to compare Steve with Troy Aikman, but I tried to plant a seed of doubt...in Steve's mind. I told reporters that Troy had won a Super Bowl and while Steve might have been an outstanding quarterback, he hadn't won one."

Johnson pointed out that when the Cowboys beat the Niners in the 1992 and 1993 NFC Championship Games, it wasn't just Aikman's passing that had allowed Dallas to light up the scoreboard. "We had Emmitt Smith, one of the great running backs of all time to share the load. With their team, in nearly every third-down situation it was all incumbent on Steve to get the job done. If he wasn't throwing the ball on third-and-short, he was running it. He had all the pressure on his shoulders.

Troy didn't have to do that because we had Emmitt."

Young's superlative six-touchdown performance in the Super Bowl did not surprise Johnson. "I would have been shocked if they hadn't won the game," Johnson said. "Every time you looked at the matchup, San Francisco's advantage looked more obvious. Rice, Watters, and Jones could win their individual battles with ease and it was just a matter of Steve picking them out. I knew he wouldn't have much anxiety because he had just beaten Dallas. It figured to be easy and it was. A great quarterback got his reward and it catapulted him into the discussion of the all-time greats."

Who would have thought that an ex-Cowboy could be so objective about a member of his team's top rival? But Johnson was sincere in his admiration for Young based on his talent, execution, and determination—and not the color of his uniform.

Young's Growth

Playing in Joe Montana's shadow had stunted Steve Young's career, statistically and emotionally. But when Young finally took over on a full-time basis in the 1992 season, he dominated the game with his accurate arm and his breakaway speed. It allowed him to open up in the locker room and speak his mind to his teammates and coaches.

"I never thought it was my team," Young said. "I didn't feel that it was my role to go around the locker room and tell everybody what to do. But once I started to play regularly, I could do that. It wasn't that my personality changed, it was that my personality could come out."

Young had played in 1991 when an elbow injury kept Montana out of the lineup for a full season, but he had shared time with third-teamer Steve Bono after a knee injury of his own had sent him to the bench.

But in the 1992 season, when Young stayed healthy while Montana was on injured reserve, he finally established himself. He completed 268 of 402 passes for 3,465 yards with 25 TDs and

Steve Young smiles as he and 49ers wide receiver Jerry Rice rush to congratulate a teammate after a touchdown against the Dallas Cowboys in November 1994. Young said of Rice, "My memory is [that] he was always open, he always caught it, and he always scored touchdowns."

seven interceptions. He also ran for 537 yards and four TDs. Despite his sensational numbers, which were recognized throughout the league as the mark of a superstar, Young could not win over the San Francisco fans, who were still enamored with the legend of Joe Montana.

Young certainly understood the fans' passion and love for Montana. Any quarterback who leads his team to four Super Bowl titles has earned the loyalty that came his way. But sometimes that loyalty was marked with disdain for Young, and it was tough for the quarterback to endure.

"It's not like I ever thought I could just slide in here without anybody noticing," Young said. "Joe did so much with this team and it was natural for people to love him and want to see him under center. But when I started it became my job."

Young's confidence grew every week. His teammates believed in him and he felt comfortable taking on a leadership role in the locker room. "Football is more a mental game than anything else," Young said. "You have to have confidence in yourself. You have to know that you can do the job. That's when your teammates have confidence in you. We made a breakthrough that year. It wasn't that players were coming up to me and telling me how good they thought I was or that I could do the job. It was a quiet and unspoken kind of thing. But in the huddle, I felt that they believed in me. When they looked at me, they knew we could get the job done."

Prior to the 1992 season, whenever Young came into the lineup he felt that he was just holding down the position temporarily and that it would ultimately go back to Montana. Since he felt his time in the lineup would be determined by Montana's availability, Young often tried to put his signature on the game by trying for the spectacular play. He would try to make the spectacular throw, even if it meant forcing the ball between defenders.

"When I got in the game, it was just for a series or two or maybe even a half," Young said. "But I felt like I had to get something done right away. That made me try to do more than I probably should have. If something wasn't there I would try to make the play anyway.

"But once it became my job and I was the regular quarterback I could be more patient. I didn't have to force the ball anymore. I could take the short dump off and wait for the next set of downs. Sometimes those five yards will mean more than the big play because it can really frustrate the defense."

Young became a better quarterback in 1992 because of his confidence, maturity, and ability. But he also benefited from the coaching of Mike Shanahan, who was in his first season as offensive coordinator of the team. Shanahan would of course go on to greater heights as head coach of the Broncos. But when he got to San Francisco and had a chance to shape Young's career, he was the perfect man for the job.

Shanahan knew that Young was a virtuoso talent and that the

only thing he would have to do with him was make a few minor adjustments. One of those was to change his thought process when he decided to run out of the pocket.

Once Young had decided to run, he became a running back, using his speed and moves to elude tacklers. Shanahan wanted him to remain a quarterback. "Just keep your eyes open as you approach the line of scrimmage," Shanahan told his quarterback. "Somebody may break loose and the big play may be there."

Young knew that, but hearing it from his coach slammed the message home. He took Shanahan's advice to heart and put some amazing performances on the board.

The 49ers had 598 yards of total offense against the Bills, put 56 points on the board against the Falcons, and led come-from-behind fourth-quarter wins over the Rams, Patriots, and Saints.

Performances like those firmly established Young as one of the best quarterbacks the game has ever seen. Eventually, his critics realized that their arguments against him had no merit. They may have loved Montana, but there was nothing lacking when Young was behind center.

But putting numbers on the board and dominating statistically was not enough for Young. He became his own biggest critic. When he completed 67 percent of his passes in a game against the Falcons, he wanted that figure to be 80 percent. That desire and hunger fueled Young's growth and would ultimately lead him to a spot in the Pro Football Hall of Fame in Canton.

The Montana-Young Clash

A fairly strong argument can be made that the 49ers had the two best quarterbacks of all time.

That's admirable for a lot of reasons. Having Joe Montana and Steve Young on a roster is evidence of the talent-evaluating ability of the scouting department, the decisiveness of the front office, and the teaching ability of the coaching staff.

It also created problems. Since only one quarterback could play at a time, Montana and Young were rivals as well as teammates.

Young dutifully held on to the number two position for years while Montana was winning championships and being celebrated as the best quarterback in the NFL (and perhaps its best ever). Young would shine whenever he had an opportunity to play, but that would not be as the Niners starter until Montana got hurt or decided to step down.

As the Niners prepared for the 1990 season, Montana had just won his fourth Super Bowl title and was enjoying life thoroughly. Step down? No way. He was the king of the NFL and was still functioning at a very high level.

But Young's frustration level was also high. He was no longer a kid. He was 29 years old and it appeared he might still be awaiting an opportunity when he was ready to retire. This could not go on much longer.

The 49ers were saved from making a decision when Giants defensive end Leonard Marshall chased Montana down at the end of the 1990 NFC Championship Game and smashed his right arm as he followed through after a pass. Young came into the game to replace Montana but could not pull out a win. A win that would have given the Niners the opportunity to go for their third straight title.

Given a full off-season to recuperate, there was no reason to think Montana wouldn't be back in the lineup in 1991. However, he felt pain in his elbow before a preseason game and that discomfort ultimately led to elbow surgery.

Young was now finally under center but there was a state of unease around the franchise. Nobody really knew if Young was now the number one quarterback or if he was just holding down the job until Montana came back in 1992.

That included Montana, Young, head coach George Seifert, his coaching staff, and any of the Niner players.

The mystery factor surrounding the quarterback position led to a divided team. How could any of his veteran teammates not support Montana? He had helped deliver four Super Bowl titles and had one miracle performance after another on his résumé.

But Montana had no more of an edge on Father Time than any

other athlete. Sooner or later Montana would have to be replaced—and no pro athlete ever had an understudy like Young, unless you go way back to Yankee first baseman Wally Pipp, who was backed up by a guy named Lou Gehrig. Unfortunately, the combination of Montana and Young on the same roster turned the Niners organization into a frothing controversy that could only end one way.

Young had an outstanding 1991 season, and he followed that with an MVP season in 1992. During that time, Montana was enduring three separate bouts of elbow surgery and the 49ers management had the good fortune of being able to turn to Young on the field.

While the move allowed the 49ers to continue to put spectacular offensive numbers on the board, it did not make the fans, the players, or the sportswriters forget Montana. As good as Young was, Montana was still their idol. Young was the better athlete with the stronger arm, but Montana was the supercool leader who always made the right decision on the field.

The love for Montana was understandable. The 49ers had largely been a losing organization prior to his arrival. The 49ers had won two playoff games since coming into the league in 1950—prior to their first Super Bowl run in 1981. Back then it was easy to get 49ers tickets, as attendance was regularly below 40,000 prior to Montana's arrival.

Montana was the face of a dramatic organizational turnaround. After they went from a 6–10 team in 1980 to Super Bowl champions the following year, the 49ers were seen as a first-class, textbook organization.

Players wanted to play for the 49ers. They elevated themselves and they elevated the city of San Francisco. Not only was the team in a major market, it was playing like it should be in one. That had not been the case before Montana.

Clearly, it wasn't all Joe. Ed DeBartolo was the owner who gave Bill Walsh everything he needed to turn the organization around. Walsh was brilliant when it came to talent procurement and organizational ability. As a coach, he was an excellent teacher and an incomparable strategist. Montana was not alone on the field either.

Dwight Clark was a classy receiver. Ronnie Lott anchored a defense that combined toughness, intelligence, and speed.

But with all of those attributes, Montana was the face of the organization and was beloved by the team's fans. So even when Young was clearly a spectacular quarterback on the field and had two football seasons with spectacular results, Montana was still the team's poster boy.

As the 1993 season loomed on the horizon, 49ers management was silently hoping that Montana would fade off into the sunset by retiring.

Montana knew that's what the organization wanted and he resented the attitude. He wanted his job back and didn't care that Young had won the MVP. He grew resentful of the organization and of Young.

The fans sided with Montana, as they always had. There was a backlash in the city and the Niners knew they had to do something.

Montana finally appeared to be healthy, and the organization completely capitulated to him. They told him he could do exactly what he wanted. He could return to the team and would be listed as the number one quarterback or he could solicit a team—even though he was still under contract—and work out a trade. But Montana thought the team was being insincere with him, that it wanted Young at quarterback but didn't have the stomach to tell him.

The Niners were taking calls about the possibility of trading Montana and the price was not extraordinary. They only wanted a third-round draft choice for him because Montana was going to be 37 years old and he had not played in two years. But when the Cardinals offered a first-round pick for Montana, the bar had been raised.

The Chiefs matched that bid and Montana liked the idea of going to Kansas City, a team that had solid weapons on both sides of the ball but lacked a quarterback. Montana decided to go to Kansas City, but before the announcement would be made publicly he flew to Youngstown, Ohio, to tell DeBartolo face to face that he had chosen to leave.

"Joe came just to tell me face to face," DeBartolo said. "I had reiterated that he would be the starter if he stayed but he just wasn't feeling it. He just couldn't accept it. He wanted to move on, and it was a rotten day for us."

Montana would be the man in Kansas City and the difference was that there would be no controversy. "If I get hurt there," Montana explained, "the fans and the organization will pray for me to get back in the lineup. They want me there."

The 49ers traded Montana, safety David Whitmore, and a 1994 third-round draft pick for Kansas City's first-round draft choice.

Montana found success in Kansas City and would have a number of memorable moments during his two years there. The Chiefs made the playoffs both seasons and he led them to a memorable road win against the favored Houston Oilers. He also engaged in one of the classic Monday night games of all time, facing off with John Elway in Denver.

The two quarterbacks engaged in a shootout during the 1994 season and Montana and the Chiefs emerged with a 31–28 triumph when he threw a last-second touchdown pass to wide receiver Willie Davis. In the game, Montana completed 34 of 54 passes for 393 yards and three touchdowns.

The departure of Montana made life easier for Young.

"Steve has been in the shadow of Montana so long, he's needed to subjugate some of his own personality," said Young's agent, Leigh Steinberg. "The hard-core Montana loyalists would react with tremendous anger to any statement that Steve was a quality quarterback or that Joe was past his prime. So Steve had to toe a very unnerving political tightrope, and knew the Montana fans were monitoring every word said by either Steve or the club executives and that any word by him would provoke some response. So Steve carefully bit his tongue for six years and stayed away from any comments."

Trading Montana allowed Young to step out from his shadow and ultimately remove one very large and annoying monkey from his back.

Playing with the Best—Rice's
Take on Montana and Young

There's no question about Jerry Rice's greatness, but it can be argued that much of his ability to make huge catches and influence games came as a result of having Joe Montana and Steve Young as his quarterbacks.

It can be easily argued that Montana and Young were two of the greatest quarterbacks in NFL history—if not the two best. However, those two men say that it was Rice who allowed them to have the opportunity to inscribe their names all over the NFL record book.

"Imagine how many touchdown passes I could have thrown if Jerry's parents had decided to have him earlier. I was a rookie in 1979 and Jerry didn't come into the league until 1985," Montana joked. "I would have had a lot more touchdowns with him."

After Montana's great run, Young took over as San Francisco's starter and Montana took off for Kansas City, where he spent the last two seasons of his career before retiring. Young threw an NFL-record 85 touchdown passes to Rice, surpassing the previous mark of 79 by Miami's Dan Marino to Mark Clayton. Their record has since been topped by Indianapolis's Peyton Manning to Marvin Harrison (107).

"My perspective is so personal because he caught my balls and made me look good," Young said. "It was magic finding someone who works as hard as you. I loved playing with him. He was so easy to throw to. My memory is he was always open, he always caught it, and he always scored touchdowns. The NFL is supposed to be hard work."

Montana still has a view of Rice that is no different from anyone else's who ever saw No. 80 play. "When you look at his stats, he's far and above everyone else," Montana said. "I think he was the best ever to play. He had a unique ability to get in the end zone and get behind you. He'd lose seven out of 10 footraces but he had the ability to get behind you. To this day I don't know how he did it."

Rice was voted Most Valuable Player of Super Bowl XXIII in Miami, but he was more dominant the next year in Super Bowl XXIV in New Orleans against the stunningly inept Denver Broncos. Rice had seven receptions for 148 yards and three touchdowns.

Although the Broncos had a season's worth of game films to analyze ("Hey, Montana throws a lot to that No. 80 guy. Maybe we should cover him.") and certainly knew what was coming, they were powerless to stop Rice, the slow-footed one who would lose seven out of 10 races. Montana was voted MVP of that Super Bowl.

"The typical example? They know what he can do and how he scores his touchdowns and yet he got behind them," Montana said of the 49ers' fourth Super Bowl championship. "If I was coaching, I'd do everything I could to stop Jerry and have everyone else beat you. I'd beat him up on the line all day."

When asked what made Rice the player he is, Montana said look no further than the club's practice fields at Redwood City and then Santa Clara.

"He has a tremendous work ethic. I talk about it all the time," Montana said. "He worked. He caught more passes [in practice] than anybody. Any time he got the ball, he ran down the field in practice. Every time he touched the ball, he scored a touchdown.

"I was blessed to have an opportunity to play with him. It's always tough to watch an athlete like him come to the end. Everyone is going to miss him going out on the field."

Referring to all the passes he threw to Rice, Young said, "We both benefited from somebody calling plays. We both benefited from a system that threw on first and second down. He was really good at getting off the line, finding seams. It was the technical part of football where we thrived."

When he was with the 49ers, Montana was regarded as one of the team's greatest jokers. As a young player, Rice was not spared Montana's mischief.

"I was always tormenting him somehow," Montana recalled. "Remember when he first had his [Fifi] hairdo? Our kids had Bert and Ernie dolls. We called him Bert because he had hair that went up like that. One time I put the Bert doll on the overhead projector and when the light went on, you could see the outline of the doll on the screen."

That was about as bad as it got, Montana said. "Nothing too harsh. I needed him to catch passes."

Chapter 11
The Other 49ers Stars

"It comes from the effort that you have given. Putting in the work and the overtime.... If you want me to go to war, I can do it and I can win the battle."

—Roger Craig

Roger Craig—The Working Man's Superstar

It was Montana's team.

It was Young's team.

It was Rice's team.

It was Walsh's team.

Nobody ever said that the San Francisco 49ers lacked for star power. But Montana, Young, Rice, and Walsh never asked for all the glory. None of them ever felt that anything less than a significant team effort could get the team over the top.

When the Niners won Super Bowl XVI over the Bengals in the Pontiac Silverdome, they had the formidable trio of Walsh, Montana, and Dwight Clark leading the way. However, the seminal moment of that game—and perhaps the start of the Niners dynasty—was a goal-line stand by the defense.

Players like Dan Bunz, John Harty, Fred Dean, and Archie Reese had as much to do with the win as any of the legends. It was an important lesson for the team and their faithful. Football has always been the ultimate team game. Superstars are nice, but they have to function within a scheme that allows everyone to contribute. Team players were ultimately just as important as the superstars.

Roger Craig was clearly a team player. He knew all about the merits of sacrificing one's own glory for the good of the team— long before he was picked by the 49ers from Nebraska in the second round of the 1983 draft.

The image of Craig and his signature style of running with his knees high is one of the lasting pictures in 49ers history. Craig was neither the fastest nor the strongest running back in the game, so he developed the style in order to make it difficult for opposing tacklers to bring him down.

But there was a lot more to his game than style. The substance was born in the off-season when Craig trained for each upcoming season. Influenced by the late great Walter Payton on the subject of training, Craig challenged himself by running the intimidating hills of San Mateo County in order to prepare for the year.

High-stepping Roger Craig gave the Niners a balanced running game and he was also a superior pass receiver.

The demanding training regimen that Craig put himself through had little to do with the start of the season. It had more to do with how he would finish each season.

In November, December, and January, when most players were battling their aches and pains and trying to survive, Craig was getting ready to kick butt.

"You build character running the hills," Craig said. "It's not just about getting the body ready, it's about getting the mind right. Once you have your thought process down and your mind is ready, nothing is going to stop you.

"It comes from the effort that you have given. Putting in the work and the overtime. Once I've done the hills, I feel like I could do anything any coach asks of me in practice. If they want me to run 20 miles I know I can do it. If you want me to go to war, I can do it and I can win the battle."

That attitude was a part of Craig's makeup long before he was drafted. Playing for Tom Osborne's Nebraska Cornhuskers, Craig had impressive ability, but so did many of his teammates. In order to stand out to his coaches—and also to visiting NFL scouts— Craig sprinted down the field every time he completed a play.

"I think that's why I got drafted where I did," Craig explained. "I had a bad ankle my senior year but when pro scouts would come and watch us, I used to sprint down the field. There was no way I was going to show them any injury or weakness. I believe that showed them something about my personality and attitude."

Any time Craig faced pain on the field, he called on the memory of his demanding off-season routine. During the 1988 season, Craig played in brutally hot games in Los Angeles against the Rams and in Phoenix against the Cardinals. When other players were feeling the draining effects of the sun and heat, Craig stoically stayed in the game and refused to recognize the impact of heat exhaustion.

"I wouldn't allow myself to get tired," he said. "It was a mental thing. It may have been boiling hot but I was not about to be defeated. The only way I was going to go down is if every other player on the field went down before me. I was in great shape.

There was no way I was supposed to be tired."

Simply put, if Craig's mind couldn't conceive it, Craig's body couldn't feel it.

By the late 1980s, Craig's reputation as a training perfectionist who kept pushing himself harder and harder had made its way around the league. In 1989, a highly touted rookie named Barry Sanders asked Craig if he could train with him and give him some tips.

Even though Sanders would play for the Detroit Lions and was in direct competition with him, Craig didn't hesitate to help. Craig had gotten assistance from Payton when he was a young player, so he in turn assisted the incredibly talented Sanders.

"I talked to him and counseled him quite a bit about what it takes to be a top back in the NFL," Craig said. "There was no doubt that he came into the league with a ton of ability and that he was one of the greatest college running backs the game has ever known. But it's a different game in the NFL because you are competing against the best players every week. It's not about maintaining where you were in college, it's about getting better."

During his 11-year NFL career, Craig rushed for 8,189 yards, scored 56 rushing touchdowns, and averaged 4.1 yards per carry. He was a four-time Pro Bowl player, he was selected the NFL's team of the decade in the 1980s, and he was named the league's offensive player of the year in 1988. He ran for a career-high 1,502 yards that season and also caught 76 passes for 534 yards.

Craig never thought of himself as a superstar and he believes the primary reason he excelled in the NFL was his capacity for hard work.

"Where would I have been without the training routine I had and the work I put in during the off-season," Craig asked rhetorically. "I would have been an average running back. That's why I never got out of shape. That came from Walter Payton. He always told me to work hard, train hard, and play physical. If I did those things, I would never get out of shape."

Craig understood those lessons well and his effort to live them made him one of the greatest running backs in 49ers history.

Not bad for an "average running back."

When Roger Craig was drafted in 1983, he saw lots of opportunities in the red, gold, and beige uniforms he would soon be wearing.

"The running backs weren't really established and so I thought this would be a great opportunity," Craig said. "And to play in Bill Walsh's system was incredible. It's a dream come true. Some of the things that he asked of his players, to be an all-purpose type of runner, I thought I fit in perfect for the system.

"I didn't come in boasting like I was a hotshot rookie trying to let everybody know who I was. I worked hard in practice and I listened to the veteran guys like Ronnie Lott and Hacksaw Reynolds. I took pride in following their lead and never questioning their lead."

Craig got an introduction into what life in the NFL was like in his first preseason game against the Raiders.

"Defensive end Lyle Alzado picked me up and slammed me down on the ball. It separated my rib cage. I couldn't run and my ribs were like a gate that kept opening and closing with the wind. For three weeks, I didn't do anything. Bill waited [until] the last preseason game against Seattle to play me and I had a great game. I ran the ball really strong.

"We didn't win, but Bill said in front of all my teammates, 'Well, we might not have won the game, but we sure found a runner. Roger Craig did a great job.' Right then and there, that gave me confidence. I knew I got the respect from my coach and from my teammates."

Craig started at fullback and he was teamed with veteran Wendell Tyler. Craig led the team in all-purpose yards. In his second year, Craig led the team in receptions and helped the 49ers win the NFC title and meet Miami in Super Bowl XIX. He scored three touchdowns on that Super Sunday as San Francisco dumped the Dolphins, 38–16.

"They had just won a Super Bowl two years before I got there, so here I am on a world-class team that knows how to take it all the way. A lot of guys said don't be distracted from the media, from your family, or from all the endorsements, just focus on the game," Craig said. "Hacksaw told me, 'Play this game like it's your last game ever because you never know if you're ever going to come back. You have to make sure you lay it on the line. You don't want to go through life saying that you didn't give it your all! I was focused and dedicated to get the job done."

The following season, Craig got the job done and more. He carried the ball 214 times for 1,050 yards and led the league with 92 catches for 1,016 yards, becoming the first player in NFL history to top 1,000 yards in both categories in the same season. Craig's outstanding performance earned him the first of his invitations to the Pro Bowl.

"We had our ring ceremony [for the Super Bowl XIX victory] and I can remember standing in line with my wife at the Palace of Fine Arts. Bill Walsh was standing there and he said, 'Roger, we expect some big things from you this year. You've got to get 1,000 yards.' Here I am a fullback, still blocking for Wendell Tyler. I said, 'All right, coach, I'm ready! I'm ready to go!' I got goose bumps when he said that. I'm like, I've got to get that 1,000 yards! But I didn't know in what category. Was it 1,000 yards for receiving or rushing? So to cover my butt, I did both," said Craig.

Pass-Rushing Phenom—Charles Haley

Charles Haley was about the most anti-49ers Niner the team has ever had.

We're talking image. The team that was identified by the West Coast offense and sophistication also had a healthy dose of the Neanderthal gene during its championship era. Ronnie Lott provided quite a bit of the mayhem, but nobody was more intimidating than defensive end Charles Haley.

Haley was probably the equal of Dick Butkus, Ray Nitschke, Deacon Jones, Bubba Smith, and Chuck "Concrete Charlie" Bednarik when it came to intimidation. We're not talking about individuals who would scare the average man walking down the street. We're talking about people who could force the toughest NFL players to lose control of their bodily functions.

Haley may be at the head of the class. You can be sure he is sitting in the front row.

If you need convincing, let's go back to the 1992 training camp. Haley was in his final days with the team after six years. Bill Walsh had drafted him out of tiny James Madison University in 1986 and Haley was extremely loyal to Walsh for taking a chance on him. However, after Walsh left, following the team's 20–16 win over the Bengals in Super Bowl XXIII, he never had the same kind of rapport with George Seifert and those feelings gradually degenerated into total disrespect.

He grew increasingly angry with the organization after his good friend Ronnie Lott was allowed to leave via free agency following the 1990 season. By the summer of '92, Haley simply couldn't take it anymore.

He wanted to leave and he did everything he could think of— and then some—in order to make the 49ers see his point of view.

Haley had no intention of going to the media and stating his case. Instead he took action against his teammates and coaches. The most well known of those actions came as Haley was preparing to leave training camp. He came upon a brand-new BMW owned by teammate Tim Harris, who had joined the 49ers the previous season.

Haley did not like Harris and decided to make his feelings for his new teammate known to everyone in the training camp parking lot. Haley climbed atop the car and urinated all over the vehicle.

Harris immediately went to confront Haley, but the battle was short-circuited because Harris had the demeanor of a human being while Haley appeared to have the persona of a crazed junkyard dog.

There were no apologies forthcoming from Haley. Instead, he continued his reign of gross behavior at a position meeting the next day.

Finally the 49ers could take no more, and they decided to trade Haley to the team that gave them the best offer.

A good idea—except the highest bidder was the Dallas Cowboys.

The move would change the balance of power in the NFC and give Jerry Jones the upper hand over the 49ers. The Cowboys were a talented and athletic team with an explosive offense and a solid defense. However, they lacked a consistent pass rush...but when they acquired Haley that was no longer the case.

Cowboys coach Jimmy Johnson was thrilled to be able to pick up a player with Haley's game-changing ability but he was also aware of the circumstances that forced the Niners to get rid of him. Johnson and Dallas defensive coordinator Dave Wannstedt sat down with Haley to find out what kind of player they were getting. Would he be the dominant pass rusher he had been in San Francisco or was he more interested in wowing his new teammates with his excretory talents?

"I remember the first time we stat down with Charles," said Wannstedt. "He said, 'I want to be treated like everyone else. No different.' He came in here and was outstanding from day one. Nobody practiced harder. He came in and he learned the scheme. He was a pleasure to work with and he made the defense a much better unit."

Haley's naturally dominant personality had a very positive impact on the Cowboys. While he never said anything threatening to his teammates, his presence on the field created the perception that he would not hesitate to let a teammate know how he felt about a poor practice effort.

"He pushed everybody," said Cowboys offensive tackle Erik Williams, who lined up against Haley every day in practice. "Haley is something else. He made me a better player. The way he practiced and the way he prepared was intense. After a week of practicing against Haley, I was ready to take on anybody."

With Haley on the roster, Dallas went on to win three of the next four Super Bowls, defeating the Niners in the '92 and '93 NFC Championship Games (and losing to the eventual champions, San Francisco, in '94), as Haley became the first and only NFL player to earn five rings.

The Niners might have been able to win another championship or two had they found a way to keep Haley. Instead, his immature and insulting behavior forced them to make a trade they would later regret. At the very least, if they had traded Haley to a team other than the Cowboys they would have been better off.

Walsh was among Haley's biggest supporters and never would have traded the star. Of course, Walsh was not with the team when Haley went on his training camp rampage.

"Charles is one of the greatest players of our era," said 49ers vice president/general manager Bill Walsh. "At one point he was considered the best pass rusher in all of football. He's been a credit to the game and very well could be a Hall of Fame candidate."

Haley seemed to play his best when his team needed him most. In Super Bowl XXIII he recorded six tackles and two sacks as the 49ers defeated Cincinnati. In Super Bowl XXVII Haley recorded six tackles to lead the Cowboys over the Bills. After having off-season back surgery following the 1993 season, he returned to the field and posted six tackles, one sack, and nine quarterback pressures in a key Thanksgiving Day victory against the Green Bay Packers. Late in the 1995 season, Haley missed five games after suffering a disc injury in his lower back. Showing his competitive spirit, he returned to the starting lineup in Super Bowl XXX and recorded five tackles, one sack, and three quarterback pressures to earn his fifth Super Bowl championship.

Haley retired from the game in 1996 with a back injury after playing in five games for Dallas. He made a triumphant return to the field in the 1998 postseason, appearing as a pass rush specialist for the 49ers in their dramatic victory over the Green Bay Packers.

It would be his last moment of glory on the field and it was just one more reason why Niners and Cowboys fans would never forget him.

Going into the 1986 draft, Bill Walsh wanted to give his pass rush a bit of new blood. Fred Dean and Dwaine "Pee Wee" Board were past their prime and if the 49ers were going to have an upper-echelon defense to go along with their world-class offense they had to find a great pass rusher.

Walsh gave the assignment to his scouting department and the job fell to a young scout named Mike Lombardi. Lombardi was given a list and told to break down all the pass-rushing defensive ends. Lombardi looked at film and read scouting reports on every name on the list and then some. He came across Haley and some highlight film from his career at James Madison. Haley stood out throughout the film session; he seemed just a bit quicker, stronger, and more explosive than everyone else.

Still, there wasn't anything that Lombardi could point to until he saw a tape of one of Haley's late-season games.

In that film, the Dukes were playing against a team running an option offense. Haley came from the backside and was just about to bring down the quarterback as he ran parallel to the line of scrimmage. The quarterback knew he was going down, so he pitched to his running back as Haley was beginning to dive. But the defensive end righted himself as he saw the quarterback pitch the ball. Haley regained his balance and took off in the direction of the running back. It was a successful move, as Haley registered the tackle that resulted in a six-yard loss.

Walsh was hoping to see something that would get his attention when he sat down in the film room, and that play did. He ran it back a couple of times and told the assembled scouting department that Haley was the kind of player the Niners needed. He had made up his mind on the basis of that one play.

The scouting department didn't like snap judgments based on one or two highlight film plays, but Walsh didn't care. He had a mind-set that if a player could make a great play once he could be taught the other aspects of the game and then make the great play again.

Defensive line coach Bill McPherson liked what he saw of Haley on film and gave Walsh the thumbs-up. They picked him in the fourth round of the 1986 draft and made him a hybrid defensive end/outside linebacker. Haley played strong-side linebacker on running downs and put his hand on the ground and rushed the quarterback in probable passing situations.

Haley went on to have a brilliant career with the Niners and he was at his best when Walsh was in charge. Haley always had a strong degree of loyalty to the man who drafted him, and he paid Walsh back by bringing it on an every-game basis during the Walsh regime.

What Others Say about Charles Haley

"Charles Haley is one of my favorite players of all time because of the way he played. Everything he did was about winning. And he's one of the greatest pass rushers ever to play the game. He was relentless and he would take the inside. So many pass rushers like to stay on the outside, but Charles would take the inside and that's what made him such a great pass rusher. In football, you are measured by how you do as a team and he is the only guy ever to win five Super Bowl rings. I think that speaks for itself."

—John Madden

"Charles Haley is one of the greatest warriors I ever played with, he is responsible for our last two Super Bowl rings!"

—Ronnie Lott

"In my opinion, we would not have experienced the run of success we enjoyed here if it were not for Charles Haley's contributions. He brought a championship attitude to our club and helped show us what it took to reach the top. I always admired and respected the way he came to play every game, every down."

—Troy Aikman

"Charles is one of the best defensive linemen I've ever played with. He was a technician and full of wisdom on football. I enjoyed playing with him."

—Emmitt Smith

"Charles had a great combination of strength and speed. He wasn't the biggest guy out there, but he had that combination and was incredibly smart on the field. You had to be prepared to play him. I certainly congratulate him on a great career."

—Anthony Munoz

Jesse Sapolu and the Offensive Line

How many times have football fans heard announcers talk about the importance of the offensive line?

"No matter how talented your skill position players are, you can't do a thing if you don't get the blocking" is the normal mantra.

Many of these analysts are ex-players or former coaches who know this to be true. But then for the next three hours of the broadcast, 95 percent of the conversation is about the skill-position players.

The 49ers have had more great skill-position players than any team, particularly at quarterback (Joe Montana and Steve Young) and wide receiver (Dwight Clark, Freddie Solomon, Jerry Rice, John Taylor, and Terrell Owens), but if they hadn't had the blocking, they never would have shined so brightly.

One of the best of their blockers was Jesse Sapolu, who was drafted in the 11th round from Hawaii in 1983. He played with the Niners through the 1997 season at left guard and center and was one of the mainstays of the offensive line. He had the perfect blend of athleticism, intelligence, guts, and toughness to fit Bill Walsh's and (offensive line coach) Bobb McKittrick's system.

But it almost never happened. Sapolu's career was an injury-plagued mess in the early years. He played in every game as a rookie and made a solid contribution to the 49ers offensive line rotation. The Niners lost a memorable 24–21 decision to the Redskins at the end of the 1983 season, but it was clear that Sapolu was a player on the rise.

But before Sapolu could assert himself and win a starting position, he fractured his right foot prior to the 1984 season. He didn't recover until the 11th game of the season against the Cleveland Browns, but he broke that same foot again the next week in practice. After an off-season of intense rehab, Sapolu came to training camp snarling and ready to play. But he suffered yet another broken right foot and missed the 1985 season.

Two years with virtually no action didn't stop Sapolu. He rehabbed once again, but he broke his left leg in training camp in

1986 and was placed on injured reserve. Many thought that was it for Sapolu. Only one game of action in three seasons had him upset, worried, and feeling more than bit sorry for himself.

Enter McKittrick, who came to the hospital to bolster Sapolu's spirits. Sapolu told McKittrick that he was thinking of going back to Hawaii and looking for a "civilian" nine-to-five type of job.

McKittrick told him to forget that idea. The late coach (McKittrick died in 2000) told Sapolu that he was a big-time player in the league and would be a legitimate contributor if he made the effort to recover trom yet another injury. "If you have the heart to fight back from this injury, I'll be there to develop you into the player I know you can become," McKittrick said.

Those words bolstered Sapolu. He recovered from the broken leg, rehabbed to get back to full strength, and became the team's starting left guard in 1987. He played the position through the 1988 season before moving to center in 1989. He became a Pro Bowl player for the first time following the 1993 season, and every time the subject of the top offensive linemen in the league was brought up for discussion, Sapolu's name was prominently mentioned.

He learned all the nuances of the position from McKittrick and learned to build his game with his own attributes. He felt that he was as strong as most of his peers on the interior line but that his advantage would be his quickness and athleticism. "I looked at the best centers in the game during that era and I saw Dwight Stephenson [Dolphins], Jay Hilgenberg [Bears], and Bart Oates [Giants] and they all relied on their quickness to help them do the job.

"The other thing I tried to do was make sure I hit the other guy before he hit me. By that I mean that I must snap the ball and take a step at the same time instead of snapping the ball and then stepping. That's one thing I worked at all the time. In the off-season, in the season. That timing had to be just right."

Switching from guard to center was a significant issue for Sapolu. He had grown comfortable at guard, and snapping the ball and making the line calls brought about a whole other set of responsibilities.

"I was comfortable playing left guard and we were coming off a season in which we beat the Bengals [in Super Bowl XXIII]," Sapolu said. "I wasn't interested in changing positions but it was best for the team. At first it was tough and restrictive. At guard I was able to pull and get out on the run a lot more than I did at center. But that always remained one of my strengths and Bobb and the other coaches still realized that.

"Before our divisional playoff game against the Vikings in 1989, they decided to let me pull from the center position. I think I became the first center to pull on running plays. It worked for us and it made the position more enjoyable for me."

One of the big keys to Sapolu's overall success in the NFL was lining up against Michael Carter and Dana Stubblefield every day in practice. Carter had been one of the strongest players in the league over the last 20 years and Stubblefield was quick and active and helped keep Sapolu focused.

Going up against those two gave Sapolu confidence when facing big-time opponents like Jerry Ball of Detroit or Keith Millard of Minnesota. In the 49ers playoff win over the Vikings in 1988, Sapolu was often pitted against Millard, who was coming off a sensational season in which he made his first Pro Bowl and had 8.0 sacks. While the numbers were good, they didn't tell the whole story with Millard. If the game was played at 100 miles per hour, Millard was going twice that speed. He was a 6'6", 260-pound mountain of energy and was one of the most intimidating players in the league. The 49ers handled the Vikings, 34–9, in that game but it was anything but easy for Sapolu. "He was an absolute beast," Sapolu said. "It took everything I had to battle that guy. He was impossible to control."

The following week the 49ers went to Chicago to play the favored Bears in the NFC Championship Game. After going through the gauntlet against Millard, Sapolu was right back in with the league's heavyweights against defensive tackles Dan Hampton and Steve McMichael. The 49ers also had to play in Chicago's brutal weather, which was in the single digits and well below zero with the windchill. Instead of folding up in the so-called Bear weather, the Niners rolled up their sleeves and beat Chicago

28–3. Neither McMichael nor Hampton ever got close to quarter-back Joe Montana.

In the locker room after the game, the 49ers warmed up and reflected on their win. When asked how the offensive line was able to control the vaunted Bears' pass rush, Sapolu said it was "difficult because they are such great players."

But when pressed, Sapolu admitted that playing against Millard the week before had been a much more difficult assignment. "Nothing against Hampton and McMichael," Sapolu said. "They are great players. But Millard was a different kind of player. If we were able to survive against him, there was no way this going to be as difficult."

Sapolu's consistency allowed him to survive through the 1997 season. He was well known in football circles as one of the best blockers on one of the best offensive lines in NFL history, but he was philosophical about truly getting the recognition that could have come his way.

"Play on the offensive line often goes unnoticed," Sapolu said. "That's the nature of the game and the nature of the position. We are not visible in the open field. What we do is very important and there is a very fine line between being a great player and being average. That's why it was so important to keep working every day—even if you had already reached some level of success. That's what I tried to do every day that I had the privilege of putting on a uniform."

His attitude was confirmed by consistent performance throughout his 15-year career.

Tom Rathman: A Fullback for the Ages

The most basic element of offensive football is not running or passing. It is blocking. Why are Joe Montana, Steve Young, Jerry Rice, and Roger Craig all considered to be among the elite players in the game's history? Certainly talent plays a key role, but solid and consistent blocking is at least as important as God-given talent.

Getty Images

Tom Rathman may not have had huge rushing totals, but he was an explosive blocker who was appreciated by his teammates and coaches. Here he breaks multiple tackles during a playoff game against the Los Angeles Rams at Candlestick Park in 1990. The 49ers won 30–3.

Tom Rathman knew that his role with the great 49ers teams in the 1980s and '90s was blocking. At least that was his primary responsibility as a fullback in the West Coast offense.

Rathman was drafted out of Nebraska in 1986 and was immediately placed in the backfield next to Roger Craig, another former Cornhusker. Rathman was a solid runner and receiver, rushing for 1,902 yards, averaging 3.7 yards per carry, and scoring 26 touchdowns. He also caught 294 passes for 2,490 yards and eight more touchdowns. He was functional and steady. Definitely not fancy.

But his primary job was blocking for Craig, Montana, and Young.

"I considered myself to be an extension of the offensive line," Rathman said. "So I had to know who I was going to block and where I was going to block."

Rathman was a part of two Super Bowl championship teams, but his favorite moment as a Niner was the team's win over the Bears on the road in the 1988 NFC Championship Game.

It was a brutally cold January day in Chicago where the wind-chill reached minus-26 degrees at kickoff. The 49ers were supposed to turn into human icicles along windy Lake Michigan. The Bears, who lived in this kind of weather, were supposed to pulverize the "soft" Niners.

Chicago area talk-show hosts and columnists had ridiculed the idea of a team from San Francisco coming into Chicago during one of the harshest winter days and doing anything but panic. An easy Bears win was expected. Not because the Bears were the behemoths that had captured Super Bowl XX, but because they were from Chicago and therefore they were "real men" and able to deal with the elements. The 49ers? They were soft and weak. They would shatter like glass when they hit the frozen Soldier Field turf.

Once the game started, it was as if perception had switched jerseys with reality. The 49ers were single-minded in their effort was sensational. They shrugged off the cold and the Bears struggled with both the weather and the competition. It was all San Francisco from start to finish as the Niners emerged with a 28–3 road victory that paved the way for a triumph in Super Bowl XXIII over the Bengals.

"That game stands out because we were able to go into that atmosphere and dominate," Rathman said. "There was no question who was going to win that game. The writers, the media—they had their own ideas about the outcome of that game, but we had no doubt. If you ask the Bears they would probably say there was nothing flukish about that game, either."

Rathman's assertion was correct. After the game, Chicago head coach Mike Ditka was seething about his team's blown opportunity. However, he knew what had happened. "We got whipped out there," Ditka said. "They came in here and outplayed us with everything on the line. They beat our butts."

Nearly 20 years after that game, Ditka's immediate assessment had not changed. "In our minds, we were the better team and we were going to win that game," Ditka said. "That was until we started to play. They won that game in every phase. Including coaching. Bill [Walsh] was simply a great coach and he came up with a winning game plan and their players executed. Period. Plain and simple. End of story."

After that win, the Niners went on to the Super Bowl against the Bengals. With the Niners trailing 16–13 in the final minute, Rathman and Craig were on the field as Montana attempted to drive the Niners downfield for the winning touchdown.

The Niners negotiated down the field successfully and were at the Cincinnati 10 with 39 seconds to play. Inexplicably, the pair of ex-Cornhuskers lined up incorrectly and executed the wrong play. Disaster was looming, but Montana rescued them by getting rid of the ball quickly to secondary receiver John Taylor, who had broken open in the end zone.

"Yes, we had a mix-up in the backfield," Rathman explained. "But if you look at it carefully, it created a window for Joe to make the throw. He delivered it perfectly and we got the win."

Rathman, who has been coaching in the NFL since 1997 (with the Niners, Lions, and Raiders), has hopes that he may one day be a head coach in the league. If he ever reaches that goal, it's clear he will be a perfectionist. He is a demanding boss and that's no different than the persona he had as a player. While he was an important player on a great team, the tough losses stand out as much as the wins because he has a hard time letting go.

During the 1989 season, the Niners went 14–2 and defended their Super Bowl championship with a devastating 55–10 win over the Broncos. However, Rathman remembers a Week 4 loss to the Los Angeles Rams, 13–12.

The Niners had a 3–0 record and led the Rams 12–10 in the fourth quarter. It was the Niners' first home game of the season and the fans were getting ready to celebrate. The Niners were trying to salt the game away with a long, clock-eating drive and Montana stuck the ball in Rathman's belly. He fumbled for only the second time in four seasons. The Rams recovered, drove 72 yards in the final minutes, and closed out the game with a field goal to win.

"We lost only two games that season," Rathman said. "We went on to win the Super Bowl, but it's hard to forget when you are the reason your team lost. We called that game 'Black Sunday' in my house for a long time."

While that game stands out to Rathman, it's his effort, intensity, and effectiveness that stand out to his teammates. "Tom was just the quintessential fullback," said Roger Craig. "I got to run the ball and he did the bulk of the blocking. I always said he could have done the running and the catching as well. He was a great football player and a sensational teammate."

A Pair of Tight Ends—John Frank and Brent Jones

The West Coast offense has been the prevalent attack in the NFL since Bill Walsh made it a staple during his run with the 49ers. The offense is reliant on the quarterback to find open receivers with short, accurate passes and put its opponent on his heels.

The best way to do this is to make use of every talented player on the field—not just one or two superstars.

Of course it helps to have a superstar like Jerry Rice and great players like Dwight Clark and John Taylor, but proponents of the offense say the key to making it effective is having a tight end who is smart, aware, and reliable to help the quarterback out in difficult situations.

If that is the case, the 49ers were fortunate to have two excellent tight ends during their Super Bowl era. John Frank and Brent Jones gave the 49ers a huge edge on their opponents on a weekly basis. Neither man was a great athlete by NFL standards, but they were mirror images of each other and matched exactly what Walsh wanted from his tight ends.

"The ideal player for the position can block for both the run and the pass and has great intelligence and he is always aware of the situation," Walsh said. "The tight end has to have an instinct of the moment the quarterback has to turn to him when the play breaks down. He also has to know how to get open and run precise patterns."

Both men did this to Walsh's exact specifications.

Frank came first, drafted out of Ohio State in 1984 and playing through the 1988 season. It was a relatively short five-year run that ended when Frank opted to leave to go to medical school. That option is not open to most NFL players.

As a youngster, his parents were against him playing organized football, thinking the game was too dangerous and that he would get hurt badly. But Frank had an ace in the hole. His grandfather was a big fan of the game and his parents told him that if Joe Frank approved of the equipment he was using and considered it safe and protective, he would get his chance to play.

"I had to show them the equipment I was wearing every day. I had to show my grandparents. I had to get permission from my father's father," said Frank about his days as a pee wee football player.

"I remember that like yesterday, going to Joe Frank's apartment in Pittsburgh and unveiling all the padding we wore. I thought it was a joke, but he was a tailor. He examined and inspected how the thigh pads fit into the pants and seams and the thickness of the padding. My father always looked at the helmets. And I think my mother was terrified by the whole experience."

Frank became a star tight end in high school and earned a scholarship to Ohio State. Playing for the Buckeyes is a tremendous opportunity for any football player with hopes of extending his career to the pro level, but that had little to do with Frank's choice. His primary career aspiration was to become a doctor, and Ohio State's outstanding medical school and cancer hospital were his primary reasons for going to Columbus.

Frank did not have huge numbers with the Niners—he never caught more than 26 passes in a season—but he won Walsh over with his ability to get open and get in sync with Montana.

Frank came off the bench for most of his career, but he won the starting job in 1988 and appeared to be entering his prime. But he went to Walsh and told him that he wanted to retire and go to medical school. Frank thought he could still be an effective player, but he wanted to retire "a year too early" instead of a year too late.

Walsh understood completely and agreed with that philosophy. He never wanted to have players stay with the team when they were no longer effective. While he was a compassionate man, Walsh was dispassionate when it came to making personnel decisions. Players who had won games for him and made big plays were always appreciated but not necessarily invited back if Walsh thought they were on the downside of their career.

As a result of Frank's decision, he became one of Walsh's favorite players. Still, the football world was shocked that Frank would leave such a great team and tremendous opportunity behind.

"Most Jewish boys growing up on the East Coast wanted to be either doctors or lawyers or accountants, and I liked the sciences. I aspired to be a doctor, to make my mother proud," said Frank, who is now a cosmetic surgeon in San Francisco.

"It had taken me four years to break into the starting lineup, and so once I made the starting lineup, that was sufficient. I was ready to retire," he said. "Before that Super Bowl season, I talked it over with some friends. I told my mother, and of all people—the irony—she suggested I play one more year. It'd taken this long to get on the starting team, so why retire now?"

Frank is thankful he took his mother's advice—and confesses that it was hard to watch his former mates roar out to a 17–2 record and second consecutive Super Bowl the year after he retired. But he doesn't regret hanging up his helmet at 27.

Frank saw 10 of his teammates go down with catastrophic injuries throughout his career, and each time it happened he realized he was playing Russian roulette with his life.

"Every time I saw something horrible happen, I realized it could have been me," Frank said. "For that reason, I was thrilled to retire. I think most players share a similar sentiment. It's really scary, especially as I learned more and more in medical school. I think most players block it out of their conscience," said Frank, who earned his medical degree from Ohio State in 1992.

Brent Jones, Fantasy Football Geek

Jones always was accessible to the public and the press. Not only did he provide great quotes to reporters, he seemed to enjoy the give-and-take with the media.

In the summer of 1994, Jones found himself thumbing through the pages of football bible *Pro Football Weekly's* kickoff issue. In that edition, the editors published their fantasy football mock draft, an avocation that would eventually sweep the nation but was then in its early stages.

I was an editor of that paper at the time and I selected Jones with my pick in the fifth round. I was the first person to take a tight end and I was chided by my "expert" peers for picking a tight end too soon in the draft. Nevertheless, I was thrilled to get Jones.

Three days after the paper came out, I came into the office and found a voice-mail message. "Steve, this is Brent Jones of the 49ers. I just wanted to tell you how happy I was that you picked me and made me the first tight end drafted in your fantasy league. It means a lot to me."

I was incredulous at the message. I didn't believe it for a second, thinking that one of my fellow editors or a civilian (non-journalist) friend had pulled a pretty funny joke. So I checked it out. I called our 49ers correspondent and played the tape for him over the phone. He told me he wasn't sure it was Jones, but that it sounded a lot like him. Then I played the tape for the 49ers media relations director and he confirmed it was Jones's voice.

I called Jones back and thanked him for his interest. He couldn't have been more friendly and it turned out to be a great pick for me. Jones finished the 1994 season with 49 catches for 670 yards and nine touchdowns. He played a huge role in my domination of the fantasy league.

More than anything, I realized fantasy football was about to become a huge phenomenon. If an All-Pro NFL player took the time to contact a sportswriter who selected him in his fantasy draft, there was no way the game could miss.

"What I really feared was a neck injury. All it takes is one fluke collision for a career-ending or life-threatening injury to occur. You realize how fragile football players really are."

When Frank retired, Jones stepped right in and became an even more effective player. He had been drafted by the Steelers out of Santa Clara in 1986, but a car accident had left him with a neck injury and he became a free agent. He signed with the 49ers and played behind Frank to understand the 49ers system. He got his chance as a starter after Frank retired and made the most of it.

He became a three time All Pro and a four time Pro Bowl player, proving to be one of the most sure-handed pass catchers in the league at any position. Jones ran all out on every play and never shied away from contact. As a result, he took more than his share of hard hits from kamikaze-like defensive backs who dove at his legs and ankles when he got into the open field. The result was some highlight-film hits with Jones often being knocked up in the air, head over heels.

But he would bounce up and come back for the next play. Jones proved quite durable despite his reckless style, playing 10 or more games for 10 straight years and playing all 16 games in four of those seasons.

Jones built a special rapport with Steve Young, as the two were roommates on the road. The night before a game he would often lobby Young to get more passes. "Yes, I would get in his ear from time to time," Jones said. "I don't think it ever really made a difference. Steve threw to the open man."

Jones's best season was in 1993, when he caught 68 passes for 735 yards and three touchdowns. He was an All-Pro for the second straight season, but he remained humble despite his lofty status.

Jones, Young, and the 49ers had an incredible season in 1994, when the Niners rallied after a slow start, won the NFC West, and finally defeated their archrivals from Dallas in the NFC championship.

Super Bowl XXIX in Miami against the Chargers was basically a walkover. Young threw a Super Bowl–record six touchdown passes and the Niners rolled to a 49–26 victory. Jones caught two of those passes for 41 yards and it was clear how much the game meant to his roommate.

"Steve had heard nothing but criticism and questions for so many seasons," Jones explained. "There was always the issue of him following Joe [Montana] and trying to get the 49ers back to the top. With the expectations that our fans and our team had, the only thing that mattered was the Super Bowl—and winning it. He did that in a huge way. I was happy for myself, my teammates, our fans, and our coaches. But I was really happy for him, considering how much he had gone through."

Jones continued to play through the 1997 season, battling through a number of injuries. In the 49ers' 38–22 divisional playoff win over the Vikings, Jones suffered a torn calf muscle.

Head coach George Seifert said it was a "season-ending" injury. Jones was in tremendous pain, but he was not about to sit as the 49ers hosted the Packers in the NFC Championship Game. Jones gutted it out and strapped on his uniform one more time, but the Niners lost 23–10 to Green Bay.

Jones called it a career after that, moving on to the broadcast booth and with a strong interest in politics. He has moved on from his football career, but he still misses the opportunity he had in competing for one of the elite franchises in sports history.

"Nothing replaces the special opportunity to play professional sports," Jones said. "I do miss it. I miss the thrill of coming out of the locker room. What I miss most is the relationships in that tight-knit locker room. I still have the highlights and the trophies and the memories, but I miss the bond I had with my fellow players and coaches."

Chapter 12
After Greatness, A Fall

Seifert had been with the team for many years. His message had gotten old and repetitive. It was clear the team needed a new coach.

Good-Bye George, Hello Mooch

George Seifert had a quiet yet effective run with the 49ers. After taking over from Bill Walsh, the team won Super Bowl titles following the 1989 and 1994 seasons. Both of those championship teams may have been the 49ers' best editions, and rate no worse than numbers two and three.

But Seifert had been with the team for many years, going back to his days as a defensive coordinator under Walsh. His message had gotten old and repetitive. The veteran players started tuning him out and the younger players didn't listen at all. By the end of the 1996 season it was clear the team needed a new coach.

While it was owner Eddie DeBartolo's decision, it was team president Carmen Policy who would pull the trigger. Policy had not been sitting around in the 1996 season. He knew that even though the Niners made the playoffs—as a wild-card team—and even won a playoff game against the Eagles that there was something missing from the chemistry. He had been watching Cal coach Steve Mariucci, who was in the process of building a solid offense. This came on the heels of an association with Mike Holmgren and Brett Favre in Green Bay.

Mariucci was 41 at the time and wanted nothing more than to coach in the NFL. DeBartolo and Policy took him to dinner and asked him to come on board as offensive coordinator for a year before taking over the head coaching job. The two Niners executives thought Mariucci would jump at the chance, but the young coach did not have his head in the clouds. He didn't want to be anyone's coach-in-waiting. He had taken the job at Cal to show he was worthy of being a head coach in the NFL and that's what he wanted. Mariucci told them that if they wanted him, it would be as head coach or nothing. He even shared with them a few of the names on his list of potential assistants.

Of the two, Policy was more convinced than DeBartolo that Mariucci was ready for the job. Both men realized that the longer they waited the more Mariucci would likely be on somebody else's radar. The Niners made their move, bringing in Seifert, who had

Young Steve Mariucci had an outstanding background in the passing game and helped manage the Niner offense when he took over from George Seifert. Owner Ed DeBartolo Jr. welcomed Mariucci to his head coaching position prior to the 1997 season.

been away on a fishing trip following the trying season. He had been entertaining the idea of retirement to begin with but would never have left on his own because he had $1.5 million due on the final year of his contract. Policy told him that he would not lose a dime of pay.

The Niners held back-to-back press conferences to announce the end of the Seifert era and the arrival of Mariucci.

Mariucci had the kind of personality that was perfect for leading one of the NFL's elite franchises. Even though the scrutiny was intense and the pressure was high, Mariucci remained cool and on track. He seemed to enjoy the media responsibilities without letting it go to his head.

The season started disastrously. The Niners went to the East Coast to play a young and enthusiastic Tampa Bay Buc team that was starting to get ferocious under head coach Tony Dungy. Steve Young was knocked from the game in the first quarter when he got caught from behind by defensive tackle Warren Sapp and knocked out when Hardy Nickerson's knee hit him in the back of the head.

If that was bad, it got even worse when Jerry Rice went deep in the backfield on a reverse. The Bucs diagnosed the play perfectly and smashed Rice. His knee was injured and he was done for the game.

The Niners lost the game 13–6, and there was a certain physical vulnerability to the team. Young returned and got the on the team on track recordwise, but there was no real confidence that this Niners team could get back to the Super Bowl.

They had a great night in December when Rice returned from his knee injury and caught a touchdown pass against the eventual Super Bowl champion Broncos in a 34–17 win, but the magic seemed to disappear after that.

They had the number one seed in the NFC with a 13–3 record and easily handled the Vikings 38–22 in the divisional playoffs, but they got taken to school by Holmgren, Favre, and the Packers in the NFC Championship Game. Even though the game was at Candlestick, the Niners dropped a 23–10 decision.

It was more of the same the following year. The Niners again had a fine record, finishing 12–4 and making the playoffs as a wild-card team behind the surprising Atlanta Falcons. But this team no longer had the feeling of one that could dominate the league. They had a great quarterback in Young and Rice was still a factor, although it was clear he could not separate the way he had in the past. However, there was a new receiver in Terrell Owens who began to assert himself. They also built a dominant ground game with Garrison Hearst.

But even with the offensive prowess, this team did not have Super Bowl written all over it. Not only did they lose the division title to the 14–2 Falcons, there was a super team in the Vikings on the horizon. Minnesota had the most prolific offense in the game and had finished 15–1.

How could the Niners beat either team?

There may have been confidence in the San Francisco locker room after the Niners finally beat the Packers after three playoff losses, but the rest of the NFL still had its doubts. Even though Owens had made a dramatic, game-winning catch on the final play of the game, few thought the Niners had a legitimate shot against the rested Falcons.

The experts were wrong and the 49ers were right. However, San Francisco dropped a 20–18 decision to the Falcons thanks in large part to bad luck. The key bad break was a literal one. Hearst suffered a badly broken ankle and the running game lost its bread and butter. The Niners fought gamely but ended up falling short. A week later those same Falcons would register a monumental upset, taking down the Vikings and earning a spot in the Super Bowl.

It would be the last time the Niners would be thought of as one of the best teams in the league.

The Last Hurrah

Big wins in dramatic situations had become the Niners' calling card over the years.

From "the Catch" in the 1981 NFC Championship Game over the Cowboys to Joe Montana's drive against the Bengals in Super Bowl XXIII, the Niners had long ago shown their fans that they could pull out miracles when they needed them.

More often than not, they took apart their opponents methodically and didn't need the hand of Providence to help them. However, when they took the field at Candlestick Park for their wild-card game with the Packers in 1998, they needed every break they could get.

Green Bay had beaten San Francisco in the postseason three years in a row and there was a definite feeling that Steve Young simply could not get past Brett Favre. There was no reason to think this game would be any different as the Packers went into the locker room at halftime with a 17–10 lead.

There were many things going wrong in this game, particularly with wide receiver Terrell Owens. He had no problem getting open and Young had no trouble finding him, but TO just could not hold on to the ball. It was frustrating for both the receiver and quarterback and also for Mariucci.

Instead of folding in the second half, the 49ers were charged up at the start of the third quarter. Nobody was more ready to play than Charles Haley, who pressed Favre all over the field and forced him into throwing an interception. Linebacker Lee Woodall came up with the pick and returned it 17 yards to the Packer 33. Young culminated the drive by hitting tight end Greg Clark with an 8-yard TD pass.

Two field goals by the Niners and one by the Packers had given San Francisco a 23–20 lead in the fourth quarter. But that was no more than a roadblock to Favre, who brought his team all the way back with a nine-play, 89-yard scoring drive. Favre hit wide receiver Antonio Freeman with a 15-yard TD pass and the Packers had a 27–23 lead with 1:56 remaining.

While the Niners had time to do something about it, there was no real confidence. The Packers were their tormentors and Owens had been failing throughout the game. But Young refused to accept defeat. Taking over at the Niners' 24-yard line and having all three of the team's timeouts, Young moved the team. Passing to J.J. Stokes and fullback Marc Edwards had gotten the 49ers inside Green Bay territory. After an incomplete pass and a six-yarder to Rice, Young found Terry Kirby with a nine-yard completion that gave the Niners another first down. Young hit Garrison Hearst with a short pass to the Packer 25. After the final timeout was called with 14 seconds left, Young decided to go back to his inconsistent big-play weapon: Owens.

It was a near disaster as Young stumbled on his set up in the pocket. Had he gone down, the clock almost certainly would have run out before the Niners could have gotten off a decent play. But

Young righted himself, stepped up, and lofted a perfectly placed pass to Owens.

The ball was right on target and Owens brought it into his numbers as he crossed the goal line. He was obliterated by Packers safeties Darren Sharper and Pat Terrell, but he did not drop the ball.

The Niners had a playoff win for Steve Mariucci. They wouldn't get another postseason victory until the 2002 season.

The TO Factor

After the Niners had won the Super Bowl following the 1994 season in resounding fashion over the San Diego Chargers, the team was on top of the football world. San Francisco had won five Super Bowl titles, more than any other team in NFL history.

But football is an ever-changing business and the only guarantee is that teams who don't make a concerted effort to get better will get worse.

With that thought in mind, the Niners went into the 1995, 1996, and 1997 seasons with a goal of bringing fresh talent and new blood into the organization.

In 1996, the Niners decided to take a receiver out of a small and somewhat unknown southern university. Terrell Owens of Tennessee-Chattanooga was selected in the third round of the '96 draft. Jerry Rice had been taken out of Mississippi Valley State in 1985 and the Niners had to think about finding his replacement.

Owens was as raw as any receiver the team had brought in over the previous five years and he would have been a waste of the coaching staff's time if Owens didn't have so much natural talent and potential.

Owens learned quickly in practice, primarily because he was going up against an outstanding cornerback in Marquez Pope on a daily basis. Pope went after Owens hard, and that taught the wide out how to beat the jam at the line and how to get open.

"It taught me how to fight to get into my pattern and how to

The egomaniacal Terrell Owens demanded the spotlight and his plays were often spectacular. However, he wore out his welcome with his churlish personality.

fight to get open," Owens recalled. "I learned a number of moves and the best one may have be the rip technique. When I have been able to engage the defender and then rip right through him, I can get and stay open."

Owens learned to use both his power and his quick feet in order to get open. He also learned quite a bit from Rice, who was eager to share his knowledge with a young, talented receiver. Rice let Owens know that one of his biggest assets was his ability to get off the line of scrimmage with the snap count. He taught Owens how to get off the line as quickly as possible and that enabled him to shock defensive backs with his first step.

Owens also used his basketball talent on the football field. Coaches told him to imagine he was playing one-on-one on a basketball court and that his job was to get around the defender.

The lessons all came together and Owens quickly became a game-breaking receiver. He came into his own in 1998 when he caught 67 passes for 1,097 yards, 14 of which went for touchdowns. But when the Niners hosted the Packers in a playoff game, Owens's lack of experience in big games was obvious. Steve Young was on fire that day, putting all of his throws on the money to his receivers, but the passes to Owens were hitting the ground. Not because they were bad passes, but because Owens could not hold on to anything that day.

Owens was aware of what was going on and he felt awful that he was putting his teammates in a position where they were probably going to lose. "I know everybody criticized me on that day and they were right," Owens said. "A lot of those passes were ones I normally come up with easily. I really put my team in a hole."

Midway through the fourth quarter, the Niners got the ball back with a 23–20 lead. If they could grind out a few first downs, the game would be theirs.

On a crucial third-down play, Young went back to Owens again. He beat the jam at the line of scrimmage, ran a precise pattern, and got open. Young's pass hit him right in the hands— and he dropped it again.

Owens rolled around on the ground in agony before he dragged himself off the field. The Packers took advantage of the opportunity and scored with less than two minutes to go.

The Niners got the ball back with 1:50 to play. Young continued to fire the ball and he hit Rice, J.J. Stokes, and the other Niners receivers but not Owens. With eight seconds to go in the game, the Niners had one last chance from the Packer 25-yard line. Young had not looked Owens's way on the drive, but this time he looked at TO as he called "All Go, Double Comeback."

Owens had to run up the seam and then angle toward the goal line. Owens was only thinking of having an opportunity to undo his previous errors. Young launched a perfect spiral to Owens. "I had a clear view of it and there was no way I was going to let this one hit the ground. As I jumped for it, I was around the one and the Packers had two defenders coming at me who wanted to take my head off. They could have had baseball bats with them. I was not going to back off of this opportunity."

Owens leaped, caught the ball, and took a violent double hit. Despite the force of the blow, he held on to the ball, kept going forward, and ended up in the end zone for the winning score.

Owens views that play as the turning point in his career. "One play can really mean an awful lot," Owens said. "This is an unforgiving game. One play can haunt a player throughout his career. One play can also send a player into orbit and help him become a star. When I made that catch I gained a tremendous amount of confidence in myself."

That's also when Owens became a media event unto himself, a planet named TO.

His ego took over and so did his desire for more money. He certainly had earned an increase, but when the 49ers decided to franchise him (completely within the rules), he groused and moaned even though that meant he would be earning $1.47 million per year.

"It's not that $1.47 million is not a lot of money," Owens wrote in his autobiography, appropriately entitled *Terrell Owens*. "But it was not what I was worth on the open market. Putting the franchise tag on me was going to mean that I did not hit the jackpot."

After more ugly talk from Owens, the two signs came together on a seven-year deal worth $35 million. The key to the deal was a signing bonus of $7.5 million. Owens also had the option of opting out of the deal following the 2003 season.

Owens started the 2000 season with a sense of security and a new sense of self-worth. His ego was also pumped up more than it had ever been and that fact came to the surface during a midseason game against the Cowboys in Dallas. After he scored a touchdown, he ran all the way from the end zone to the Cowboy star at midfield of Texas Stadium. Owens raised his arm to celebrate and he was roundly booed by the partisan Cowboy fans. Players were incensed on the Cowboy sidelines and it started a controversy that ended with Owens being suspended for a game.

Owens thought his team caved in to pressure from the league

and hated that they did not support him. It only increased the bad blood that Owens had for his employers.

Toward the end of the season, it was clear that Owens was now the number one option in the San Francisco offense and that he had made it above Rice in the offensive pecking order.

The Niners would have liked to see Rice fade off into retirement, but he had the heart of a champion and was not interested in retiring. Rice eventually signed with the Raiders across the bay, but the Niners did not let him go without giving him a proper sendoff. In the final game of the season, the team held Jerry Rice Day as the Niners hosted the Chicago Bears. The 49ers wanted to send Rice out with another memorable day, but it was TO who created the memories.

With the Bears doubling and tripling Rice, Owens was able to run unimpeded throughout the Bears defense. With Jeff Garcia at quarterback, Owens caught a record 20 passes for 283 yards.

In 2002, Owens found himself in the middle of another controversy. The Niners traveled up the coast to play the Seahawks on *Monday Night Football*. One of the keys for Seattle was containing TO, but he broke free from coverage and caught a touchdown pass in the first half. Instead of doing a dance or pantomiming a celebration, TO rolled up his pants leg and reached down into his sock. He pulled out a gold Sharpie pen, signed his name on the football, and ran to the first row of the stands and handed the ball to a friend of his.

The "Sharpie" celebration set off another leaguewide controversy. Seahawks coach Mike Holmgren harrumphed his way through a press conference after the game—the Niners won 28–21—and called Owens's behavior "shameful" and said Owens's act was a "dishonor to everyone who had ever played the game."

The 2003 season was a critical one for Owens. Under the terms of the deal, Owens could eschew the final three years of his deal and turn his back on $17.7 million in salary in 2004, 2005, and 2006. TO went to another Pro Bowl following the 2003 season after he caught 80 passes for 1,102 yards and nine touchdowns and decided to have his agent David Joseph opt for free agency.

According to Joseph, all Owens had to do was sign a letter by March 2 saying he wanted to test the free-agent waters. However, the league said the papers had to be in the possession of the league and the NFL Players Association by February 10.

Joseph said he had "never gotten the memo" and didn't know about the change in the collective bargaining agreement.

Joseph was being ridiculed by the media and Owens refused to part with the agent that had represented him for eight seasons. Ultimately, the Niners gave Owens and Joseph permission to broker a trade—as long as the terms were to the Niners' liking. The Baltimore Ravens and Philadelphia Eagles both wanted to make trades, and Owens liked the idea of going to a contender like the Eagles who had a fine quarterback in Donovan McNabb.

After much drama, Owens ended up in Philadelphia with a less-than-stellar financial deal. The Eagles were willing to give Owens $8.5 million up front (combined signing and roster bonus money) and a paltry $660,000 in salary. His salary the second year was $3.25 million.

At the same time the Eagles brought Owens in, they also signed free-agent defensive end Jevon "the Freak" Kearse to a contract that would pay him $20 million over the first two years of the deal with $12 million guaranteed.

This would eventually eat at Owens and cause his relationship with the Eagles to blow up, but at the time he went to Philadelphia with high hopes.

One thing was certain. His days in San Francisco were over and he was now somebody else's big-play wide out—and pain in the butt.

Niners Hire Martz

It will get worse before it gets better.

The 49ers dynasty began the day owner Eddie DeBartolo Jr. got rid of renegade general manager Joe Thomas and brought in a thoughtful, incisive, and decisive coach named Bill Walsh.

Walsh remained on the sideline for 10 years, and when he left the team stayed at or near the heights under his successor George Seifert. When Seifert was let go following the 1996 season, the franchise tried to recapture the offensive glory by bringing in Steve Mariucci from the California Golden Bears to take over.

Mariucci had great offensive insight, could communicate with his players, and had the skills to rebuild a great franchise. But only to a point.

Dennis Erickson and Mike Nolan have tried to bring the franchise back, but the 49ers have languished since the start of the 2003 season. Both Erickson and Nolan had serious credentials when they were hired, but a good résumé is not enough to return the team to glory.

Through most of the post-Walsh, post-Seifert eras, owners John and Denise York have tried to run the franchise with dignity and class. They haven't always succeeded, but at least that was a factor in their decision-making process.

At least it was until the 2008 off-season. That's when the Niners brought in Mike Martz to right the offensive ship.

Martz came to the forefront in the NFL as the architect of the Rams' powerful offense under Dick Vermeil during 1999 championship season. At least Martz was the coach who grabbed the headlines. Since wide receivers coach Al Saunders had as much to do with the development of quarterback Kurt Warner and wide receivers Isaac Bruce and Torry Holt as Martz, he could have buddied up to the media and whispered in the right ears and become "the story behind the story." Instead it was Martz.

He eventually followed Vermeil as head coach of the Rams and followed that with a disastrous stint as offensive coordinator of the Lions. Now he gets to work his brand of magic with the 49ers.

It is not a great prospect for 49ers fans who got used to champagne and caviar under Walsh and Seifert. As poorly as the food has tasted in recent years, they will now have to get used to the dog food that Martz regularly serves.

The hiring of Martz was designed by Nolan in a move to make one of the least effective offenses in the NFL exciting and vibrant. But try telling that to quarterback Alex Smith, who will be working with his fourth offensive coordinator in five years.

Martz says the pieces are in place and that "they just need to be tied together."

He promises to play the part of the good soldier and do his job and nothing else. But Martz is the opposite of a team player. Instead of caring about the good of the franchise, Martz has always cared about Martz, and that attitude has disemboweled the Rams and kept the Lions in the dumper.

Martz wants to be a head coach again. He admitted that when he was hired. "Sure I do," he replied. "But I don't know whether the opportunity will come up again."

Here's what Martz is hoping. He would like to see the Niners show enough improvement on offense that they can become a viable threat to win games consistently again. He would also like to see a defense that fails to hold up its end of the bargain.

That would mean Nolan would lose his job and Martz would become the heir apparent.

Nolan knows that he has to turn things around soon or the franchise will make another move at the top. He knows his lack of security is appealing to those with higher aspirations. He has to know that's why Martz wanted to come to San Francisco—no matter what he says publicly.

Martz is not going into the NFL's Hall of Fame, but his smugness is legend. His two Super Bowl appearances—he lost to the Patriots with the Rams in Super Bowl XXXVI after helping Vermeil beat the Tennessee Titans two years earlier in Super Bowl XXXIV—has given him the currency to think that he is smarter than anybody else in the game.

Never mind the presence of Bill Belichick, Mike Holmgren, Tom Coughlin, Tony Dungy, or Mike McCarthy.

Martz believes that he's the man.

He may be fairly innovative when it comes to offensive football, but he is even farther ahead of the curve when it comes to feathering his own nest.

Prior to the Rams' Super Bowl win, he was named the team's head coach in waiting. After the win, Vermeil retired and turned the job over to Martz. It was a move that Vermeil has said he still regrets.

The atmosphere in St. Louis turned into a storm front. Martz regularly clashed with the front office and when he took ill in 2005, he was not allowed to call in plays from home and was subsequently fired.

The results that followed in Detroit were predictable. Old-school head coach Rod Marinelli wanted the offense to run the ball frequently in order to take the pressure off the defense. Martz had no such interest. He called in pass after pass and the team collapsed in the second half of the season.

Nolan's philosophy is similar to Marinelli's. That means Martz should fit in about as well as O.J.'s glove.

Juxtapose the start of the Martz era on offense with the start of the Walsh era nearly three decades earlier and there is virtually nothing in common. The glory years have become little more than a distant memory for the Niners and their fans.